Black Holes
— and —
Energy Pirates

··

How to Recognize
and Release Them

Jesse Reeder

Gateway

Gateway
Hume Avenue
Park West
Dublin 12
with associated companies throughout the world
www.gillmacmillan.ie

Print origination by
O'K Graphic Design, Dublin
Printed by
ColourBooks Ltd, Dublin

The paper used in this book is made from the wood pulp of managed forests.
For every tree felled, at least one tree is planted, thereby renewing natural resources.

A catalogue record is available for this book from the British Library.

1 3 5 4 2

In Praise of
Black Holes and Energy Pirates

"Brilliantly clear yet warmly compassionate, Jesse Reeder's book guides us gently and inexorably to the only possible conclusion: we are responsible for our own success and happiness. If you want to leave a legacy of joy and gratitude, read this book. It will change your life."

—Mary Manin Morrissey
author, *Building Your Field of Dreams*

"Jesse Reeder dissects the ways we undermine ourselves and give our power away. I especially enjoyed her examples of people first discovering their power leaks and then finding out how to patch them."

—Alan Cohen
author, *The Dragon Doesn't Live Here Any More*
and *A Deep Breath of Life*

"Jesse reminds us that we have a choice of how we live. We can have our personal energy depleted by remaining on autopilot, or we can reach out for the possibility of greater understanding and personal peace through the tools she offers. Her willingness to reveal her own struggles and the numerous personal stories make this second choice accessible to all of us."

—Sue Hickey
former Chief Operations Officer
Bonneville Power Administration

"This breakthrough book … provides practical guidelines on how to escape from emotional quicksand in relationships, become immune to energy draining people, and consciously create a strong flow of healthy, effective energy in every aspect of your life."

—Al Siebert, Ph.D.
Author, *The Survivor Personality*

"Intellectually provocative, spiritually stimulating, and grounded in life. I highly recommend it to anyone who takes responsibility for his or her life."

—Ronald R. Short, Ph.D.
Author, *Learning in Relationship: Foundation of Personal and Professional Success*

"A very insightful book, filled with ideas and tools to enhance your life and relationships. When you put Jesse's ideas and tips to work, you will increase your effectiveness in all areas of your life."

—Leslie Smid
Organizational Development Specialist
IBM

ACKNOWLEDGMENTS

I am deeply grateful to many friends who supported me throughout the development of this book. I am also grateful to my business associates Chris Thomerson and Leslie Smid, who steadfastly supported me in developing the ideas in this book and in learning about myself. I want to thank my family, my parents, my siblings, my children, and both my former husbands, who have been my greatest teachers and who all allowed me to use their stories. I also want to thank my friends and clients who agreed to have their stories told.

The list of readers and writers who supported and encouraged me, and helped shape and edit portions of this book, is long. To these wonderful friends I send my love and deepest thanks. This group includes: Judith Aftergut, Cecelia Birckhead, Kamala Bremer, Megan Brown, Kassy Daggett, Chris Dillon, Amy Gibson, Ph.D., Lee Johnson, Ron Kerns, Carolyn Kortge, Mette Lockwood, Elizabeth Lyons, Stew Meyers, Victor Rozek, Peter Shimkus, and Al Siebert, Ph.D.

Special thanks to Dennis Obert, Dirk Swanson, and the rest of my "miracle" group, who prayed for me, supported me, and celebrated with me, meeting at my home every week for two years as this project unfolded.

I would like to acknowledge three important programs that helped shape the ideas and the concepts presented here. First is the Guided Self Healing Therapy program (GSH), which taught me how to release blocked energy. I have great admiration for the work of Andrew H. Hahn, Psy.D., who developed GSH and currently trains therapists across the country. The Innovative Learning Group in Eugene, Oregon, offering Wings Seminars, helps people see the truth about themselves in their loving and powerful personal development seminars. The Leadership Institute of Seattle (LIOS), a graduate program in Organizational Development and Psychology Counseling associated with Bastyr College in Bellevue, Washington, provided pivotal direction in developing the models and concepts which are presented here. LIOS offers a powerful combination of intellectual excellence and experiential development. I want to personally thank my teachers in these programs: Dr. Andrew Hahn, Ramsey Coolidge, and Roberta Roth from GSH; James Newton, Kris King, Rick Blair, and Bev Foster from Wings; and Drs. Ron Short and Rhonda Gordon from LIOS.

I am grateful to everyone at the Eugene Water and Electric Board. I especially want to acknowledge a few individuals whose friendship has been important and who greatly contributed to my experiences in the electric utility industry: Randy Berggren, Deb Brewer, Jim Brown, Mel Damewood, Sarah Hendrickson, Krista Hince, Gary and Eileen Kunkle, Vicki Maxon, Mat Northway, Jim Oringlosso, Keith Parks, Tom Santee, Ed Sheridan, Scott Spettel, and Don Vanderzanden.

I am especially grateful to my neighbor Barbara Scott, who listened to every word I wrote and rewrote, and made important suggestions.

Finally, I want to acknowledge my agent Sheree Bykofsky whose tireless support and encouragement introduced me to Janet Rosen, Stephanie Marohn, and Elaine Gill, whose careful suggestions and editing smoothed and crafted my manuscript into a readable, compelling book. Elaine Gill not only edited and published my book, she also taught me what to stand for and when to let go in the world of editing and publishing. I have great respect for her clarity, her knowledge, and her tenacity.

It was only with the help of all these individuals that this book took shape and was born. The creation of this book confirms the energy principles it offers. We are all connected and as such I feel privileged to call myself the author of this work.

CONTENTS

Introduction

::::::::::::::::::::::

After getting a degree in microbiology, I married my college sweetheart and got my first real job—as a biochemist at Stanford Research Institute. The future looked golden, and even more golden with the birth of our first child three years later. When my husband was accepted in graduate school at the University of Oregon, I left my job and we moved north to Eugene. We were blessed with a second child, a son, and I stayed home with the children for five years. While my husband disappeared into his studies, I carted the kids off to meetings and marches to protest the Vietnam War. When I decided to go back to school for a master's degree, my husband wasn't happy. He wanted me at home with our children, while I needed to pursue my own dreams. It was a standoff. He felt threatened, I felt limited, and the marriage began to unravel. Realizing I couldn't stay in the marriage and be myself, I moved out of the house. He challenged me in a desperate custody battle that ended with a joint custody ruling.

Even though I managed to finish my degree in urban and regional planning in the midst of this trauma, I thought my life was over. By day, I just barely held myself together, hardly recognizing the "A" student I expected of my public self. By night, I plunged into an angry, hopeless pit of despair. Fortunately, I didn't know at the time that this was just the first of the deep black holes waiting for me.

Single, bruised, and needing to support my half of the joint custody agreement, I accepted a governmental liaison job with EWEB, Eugene's water and electric utility. Putting a professional lid on my pit of despair, I immersed myself in learning about electric and water systems. I was the "A" student again; I became a workaholic and studied the managers who got ahead so I could follow their example in playing the corporate game. I played well—in only seven years I landed the chief executive's job. Remarried and on top of the professional game as head of the entire water and electric utility, I thought I now had life under control. I was sorely mistaken.

Five years later, I suffered the humiliation of being publicly fired by the elected utility board and evicted from the corporate executive suite. My second marriage was teetering as my children left for college, and I suddenly found myself back in that pit of rage and despair. This time I made myself face it: I started to write.

My mother was a poet who also wrote short stories. My younger brother is a nationally recognized broadcast journalist. I was never interested in writing—after all, I was a scientist. But now, like a dog scratching at fleas, I felt compelled to write. I wrote stories. I wrote about what I didn't understand. I wrote about what had gone wrong. I wrote about the pain that wouldn't go away. I wrote four hundred pages that took a microscopic look at that pit of fear and despair. I recognized that fear had ordered much of my life—fear of failure, fear of physical harm, fear of rejection, fear of death, fear of public speaking and humiliation, fear of being who I really was. I realized I was writing to make sense of how I had let fear rule my life.

As we struggled on the brink of separation, my second husband and I tried to keep our marriage together by exploring parts of Mexico and the South Pacific by sea kayak. These trips of extreme physical exertion and hours of quiet meditation helped me connect with a deeper part of myself, and this sustained me through these troubled times. But kayaking couldn't save our marriage. Don and I divorced, and soon after our beloved dog and cat both died. Reeling from my losses, I faced the prospect of creating a new life.

My older brother, who leads tours to ancient sacred sites, invited me to travel with him to Peru and Greece. There I awakened a mystical, deeply spiritual side of myself. A week after returning to Oregon, I sat in front of my computer to look at my reams of writing. I took several deep breaths and asked myself: "What am I trying to write? How do I describe what I am learning?"

The answers came quickly: "The combination of human action and intention is the power of creation. Human creativity can be ignited by our connection to each other, but that ignition can be smothered by our own fear, blame, and resentment. So we are plagued by two phenomena that imprison and deplete our natural creative energy: our unconscious black holes—the stories, patterns, and beliefs we hide from ourselves—and the energy pirate maneuvers—the dodging we do to disguise those black holes which results in mucky, confused contact with other human beings."

I stopped and read what I had written—black holes and energy pirates. That was it! I had been in a black hole many times, not just the extreme pit of anger and despair I experienced after my divorces and other losses, but the less intense black holes of everyday life. I also knew about my own maneuvers to disguise those black holes, the ones I call energy pirating: the uncomfortable interactions and failed personal relationships that had drained my energy. Through my suffering and my journey to understand myself, my energy was ignited now with a new focus, and this book was born.

However, it wasn't until my mother's death two years later that I fully knew why I was writing. In 1998 my mother's bone cancer spread to her lungs, and a stroke paralyzed her left side. I flew to North Carolina to be with her. When I arrived at her hospital bed, I wasn't sure she knew I was there. She could no longer see and was barely able to speak, but when I slipped my hand into hers, she tightened her grip and whispered my name. When I told her I loved her, she squeezed my hand again. I lay my head against her shoulder and wept. A year before, I didn't understand a poem she had written about how she wanted to die. I simply hadn't wanted to think about her dying.

I want to die here in my home
Where all my pictures hang.
Where love and tears have intertwined.
For lo this long, long time.

I want my children near me
And my partner of sixty years.
I'd hate to die alone
In some dreary cold gray room.

I want to die with sunlight
Through windows clear and bright,
So when the angels find me,
I'll go directly to the light.

—MILDRED E. BUZENBERG

Now I understood the poem and wanted to give her what she really wanted. When she developed pneumonia on top of everything else, my father and I talked with her doctors about the options. They expected us to make the decision whether to put her on life support systems that would prolong her life or accept the inevitable and make her remaining days as comfortable as possible. It didn't occur to them to include her in the discussion. They had forgotten that it was her life and her decision. I couldn't make the decision so I told her about our conversation with the doctors. Sobbing, I said that without life support she probably would live for no more than two weeks. "Is that what you want, Mom?" I whispered. She squeezed my hand and nodded.

It was the week before Christmas and all the airlines were booked. Through a series of minor miracles, my sister and two brothers managed to get flights and arrive within a couple of days. We brought my mother home and spent that week together, telling stories, reminiscing, holding hands, crying, singing, and praying together. She passed from this life, as she wished, at home with her family on Christmas morning.

What I learned from my mother and the painful, moving experience of her death is that even in death we create our lives. Her unwavering, clear intention, the intention expressed in her poem, and her inspiring surrender ordered the final week of her life. Later, when I could think about it, I realized that clear intention, not compromised by black holes, limiting beliefs, and energy pirates, is a very powerful creative force. I realized too that most of us can't activate our creative power consciously because our black holes are blocking our energy.

My mother's death gave me a new perspective on energy and the devastating experiences I had gone through. I saw that, painful as those losses were, they had helped me. I think we are given the gifts of tragedy, sorrow, and humiliation to help us find, accept, and release limiting unconscious patterns and beliefs from our black holes so that they no longer will rule our lives. My mother's death helped me see that the real purpose of releasing our black holes and energy pirates is to clear and expand our creative life force so that we can consciously build our lives.

In this book, I share my own story and the stories of my friends and clients in our struggles with black holes and energy pirates. My hope is that these stories and the tools I developed will help you release your black holes and avoid those energy pirates so you too can create the life of your dreams.

The ideas in this book are a work-in-progress. I believe we have much to learn about the creative capacity of human energy. I encourage you to trust yourself. You will know what to embrace and what to leave as you explore how to create your life energetically.

I offer *Black Holes and Energy Pirates* as a revolutionary model for understanding human energy and creativity. By releasing our black holes and refusing those maneuvers I call energy pirating, we can live up to our greatest potential. I believe that if we support each other in cleaning up our muddy unconscious patterns and limiting beliefs, we will create a more habitable and harmonious world. I invite you to join me in consciously creating our world by exploring the rich resources of our inner lives.

Chapter One

Human Energy Fields

· ·

One Monday evening I stood in my office on the top floor of the water and electric utility headquarters building on the banks of the Willamette River in downtown Eugene, Oregon. The darkening sky visible through the wall of windows seemed to reflect the gathering storm that had been closing in around me since the utility board election the previous year had shifted the vote against me. I used to be able to count on three out of the five commissioners. Now I could count on only two, and the swing vote was avoiding me.

It had been a stormy weekend, with the board president and a commissioner asking me privately to resign from my post as chief executive. I had refused, explaining to them that the utility board had never been in a better position: the highest bond rating nationally for an electric utility, the second lowest rates in the nation for a utility of our size, and extremely high customer approval ratings. But I knew that we had different priorities and management styles. Now I was due at a public hearing on utility rates, held in the community meeting room to accommodate the large crowd expected. When I seated myself at the board table with the five commissioners, I faced three television cameras and a bank of microphones. Looking for familiar faces in the crowd, I saw my four division directors with their teams, a number of civic leaders, a few dozen employees, and some retired employees. The rest were customers and citizens interested in the rate hearing.

The president of the board banged his gavel and called the meeting to order. The commissioner who had joined the president in requesting my resignation called for item ten on the agenda—the evaluation of the general manager—to be moved to the top of the agenda. My swing vote, the newest member of the board, seconded the motion. The board president called for a vote. Three "yeas" intoned in unison. "Three in favour, the motion passes." The second commissioner finished the announcement: "Three of the commissioners have agreed to fire the general manager, Jesse Reeder."

Sarah, one of the commissioners who supported me, slammed her hand down hard on the board table. "That motion is out of order. It is a flagrant violation of the open meetings law. If there are any valid grounds for firing someone, we should make those public." She added that collusion outside the official board meeting was illegal.

"The reason we are firing Jesse Reeder is that we have lost confidence in her ability to manage the utility," said the second commissioner. Hearing this, Sarah called for input from the staff and general manager. My other ally on the board supported her.

The board president shot back, "That won't be necessary. I call for a vote." Once he got it, he announced, "The motion has passed by three to two. The general manager is officially fired. She is to clean out her office and be off the premises by 8A.M. tomorrow morning." A second motion appointed the assistant general manager as interim general manager. It passed, three in favor of the motion, two abstaining.

I sat stunned. Silence fell over the room. Nobody moved, and time seemed to stretch into eternity. Then Sarah stood up and announced that she was leaving the meeting in protest. She marched over to me and placed her hand gently on my shoulder, "We are not wanted here, Jesse. Come with me."

As I rose from my chair, the audience rose and gave me a standing ovation. I looked at my friends standing there with tears in their eyes as television cameras and radio and newspaper reporters followed me. Then something happened that I'd never experienced before. A part of me became a detached observer of the drama I was in. I felt the mistrust of the three board members, the loyalty of my management team, and the excitement of the press.

When I stopped in the hallway, I was surrounded and bombarded with questions: Why do you think the board fired you? What does this mean for the rate increase? Was this a surprise? Why didn't you resign?

I answered their questions calmly, then turned to the employees who had gathered around us. "I am sad to be leaving the utility. My work here has been very important to me. I have every confidence in your abilities to carry on what we have begun. This utility has the distinct advantage of having some of the most talented and capable people in the industry. Your strength will carry you through."

I saw the whole process unfolding as I played my part in the swirl of what had been set in motion. The press conference over, reporters raced to telephones and computers to file the story. I was late-breaking news. I was history.

Although I did not see it at the time, this painful experience was similar to other times in my life where I helped create the experience. The gathering storm I felt that Monday evening was those influences in operation—an energy field created by all the players—an energy field riddled with fear and distrust.

My contribution to the energy field began when I first took the job. From the beginning I felt intimidated by the president of the board, and my preparation for meetings with him took on the weight of a criminal trial with me as defendant. Our confrontations left me frazzled and exhausted, and I could not change my reaction to him.

My former boss had appreciated my work. The board president didn't. Although he didn't express it, I suspect that he believed a woman couldn't do the job, especially a woman who cared about people and a healthy environment. I felt his disapproval, and it touched a fear in me that I wasn't good enough for my high-visibility job. His intention to get rid of me subconsciously fueled my fear, and my reactions to him escalated his reactions to me in an endless chain. Together, we had created an energy field of fear and mistrust that ultimately led to my public firing.

Human energy fields are full of information—information that includes our beliefs, our intentions, our emotions, our personal experiences, our histories, and our characters. This information behaves like a magnet to attract and repel personal relationships and experiences that match our fears, beliefs, and expectations. Our own energy ceaselessly influences and creates our personal experiences. We are aware of some of the information in our energy fields, but our lives are guided and influenced by patterns and information far beyond what we hold in our conscious awareness.

The more we are aware of energetic information, the more choices we have over the influences that dominate our field. If I had been unwilling to remain in an atmosphere of suspicion and distrust, I should have looked for another job. But the pattern in my energy field—to work for acceptance in a field of distrust and opposition—set me up for trying to win over opposing board members who had no intention of changing their minds.

In order to change non-productive patterns, we have to find where our personal energy is unconsciously working against us. Sometimes our energy is balled up into an unworkable mess I call a black hole. Black holes block the flow of consciously created energy by holding on to unconscious emotional stories and beliefs. In my case, as I later discovered, I was holding two beliefs: I was not welcome in a male dominated world and might not be competent in my high-level job. These beliefs were hidden in my black holes. Even though I was doing the job, even though the utility was prospering under my leadership, these beliefs persisted in my unconscious. I was not aware of them except as they showed up in my self-talk. I was constantly questioning myself: Can I do this? Am I good enough? Should I resign? The source of all this self-doubt—the experiences that went into making this black hole—was hidden from my conscious attention.

I was also unaware that what I was experiencing with the board president was what I have since named energy pirating. The board president questioned my every move with suspicion and distrust. My energy was being drained by our encounters, and I didn't know what to do about it. But I get ahead of myself. Before I tell you more about black holes and energy pirating, I want to explain a bit more about human energy and why it is important.

We Are Walking Energy Fields

Energy is a fundamental building block of nature. Scientists have concluded that at the subatomic level, particles of matter and waves of energy are interchangeable. Thus, matter is energy. Since the human body is matter, that means we are energy—fields of energy.

The densest part of the human energy field is the physical body. Imagine yourself sitting in the middle of your own atmosphere, just as the earth is sitting in its own atmosphere. The earth and its atmosphere are all one system. Your body is like that too. It is the tangible and visible part of your energy, but your energy field extends past your body, just as the earth's atmosphere surrounds the physical planet. Your energy field infuses your body with life and extends beyond your skin. The energy surrounding you is not visible to most people; if it were, they would see you glowing like a switched-on light bulb.

In the physical universe, scientists have identified four energy forces. These forces can help us understand how human energy fields work. These are the four physical energy forces: a strong force that binds particles together to form atoms, the elemental building blocks of matter; a weak force that causes atoms to emit nuclear particles; electromagnetic energy; and gravity.

Scientists can study, describe, and verify the existence of these four forces, but they can't fully explain them. Nor can they assure us that these are the only forces in the universe. In fact, scientists are currently considering the possibility of a fifth force that could account for the continuing expansion of our universe despite the forces of gravity.

Human energy, which I also call personal energy, is another energy field that we cannot yet fully explain. I believe that human energy fields are similar to electromagnetic energy. Some electromagnetic energy fields, created by a flow of electrons, are visible in the physical universe. The two most spectacular examples are lightning and the aurora borealis, known as the "northern lights."

Magnets function as a specific expression of electromagnetic energy. A magnet is a chunk of iron with positive and negative ends we call poles. A magnet draws iron or another magnet to it before it actually makes physical contact. If you place a magnet near a mound of iron filings, you can see the compelling force of its invisible magnetic field as the iron filings begin to "migrate" toward the magnet. Human energy or personal energy is like that magnetic field—a soft visible field flowing through and around us that attracts complementary patterns of human interaction just as a magnet attracts iron and complementary magnets.

Quantum experiments have demonstrated that the expectation of a researcher determines whether a subatomic particle shows up as a particle of matter or a wave of energy. When the researchers expected to see a particle of matter, that's what they found. When the researchers expected to see a wave of energy, that is what they found. Amazing as these studies are, they have been accepted by the scientific community. From this research we can conclude that pure energy manifests as particles of matter or waves of energy depending on human expectations, beliefs, and intentions. In other words, human intentions create reality at the subatomic level.

Human intentions, emotions, and beliefs are some of the formative information of human energy fields. Formative information draws experiences that match or complement our emotions, beliefs, and intentions. We are walking energy fields, attracting what we fear, hope for, intend, expect, and believe, while repelling what we don't believe, expect, or intend. In my job at the utility I drew to me someone (the board president) who matched my beliefs about myself, someone who distrusted my abilities and fed my uncertainty.

In this book, I am suggesting that it is possible through our energy fields to create and attract consciously what we want in our lives, instead of unconsciously drawing in what supports our black holes and blocks our energy. If we want to make a positive change in our lives, we must find and alter the established patterns that dominate our energy fields. That is why energy fields are important. By exploring human energy fields, understanding how they function, and exposing the secrets they hold, we can expand our creative energies and consciously build our lives.

Human energy focused with personal emotion, intention, and belief becomes creative energy—energy that has the capacity to create what we experience. We know very little about human energy fields, but our creative capacity seems to arise within our energy fields. Our creative capacity includes three groups of formative information or energy: mental, experiential, and intentional. We build our lives with these groups of formative information that interact and become our creative human energy.

MENTAL ENERGY—
THOUGHTS, BELIEFS, EXPECTATIONS, AND STORIES

Mental energy is what we expect and how we interpret and explain what happens in our lives. It includes thoughts, ideas, concepts, and mental processes such as reasoning and analysis.

Beliefs are thoughts that have been remembered or retraced many times. For example, I believed that I was not welcome in a male-dominated world. I had thought about this many times and confirmed it with my experience until it became my belief. Because we return to our beliefs again and again, they generate more creative energy than thoughts do.

Expectations are beliefs about the future. For example, I expected my work to be challenging and difficult, and my experience confirmed that expectation.

Stories are usually a way to understand and interpret our past. One story I told myself was that my brothers got my dad's attention because they were boys.

All this formative information infuses our energy field with creative energy—energy that has the capacity to create comfortable or uncomfortable experiences, depending on its content.

EXPERIENTIAL ENERGY—
FEELINGS, SENSATIONS, AND EMOTIONS

The second group, experiential energy, is our reaction to our understanding of what happens. This group includes the full range of human feelings made up of both emotions and sensations. The four primary human emotions are sadness, fear, anger, and happiness. Physical sensations include warmth, cold, tension, shakiness, fatigue, hunger, pressure, and pain. Sensations and emotions are both felt in the body, and the line between them is a fuzzy one. For example, feeling nervous can be categorized as both a sensation and an emotion.

INTENTIONAL ENERGY— INTENTIONS, WANTS, INTERESTS, AND DESIRES

The third group, intentional energy, sets the direction for our creative energies. Intentions, wants, interests, and desires direct our actions, words, and behaviors. Having a clear intention is crucial to consciously attract what we want. We may have hidden (unconscious), conflicting desires that confuse or thwart our conscious intentional energy. Intentions concentrate our energy to create our desires—like focusing the sun's light through a magnifying glass to start a fire.

The three groups of formative information interact with and influence each other. We react emotionally to our mental understanding of what is happening. If we change our understanding, our emotions change. For example, if we believe that someone has harmed us, we may feel angry. If we later realize that he actually helped us, we may feel relieved or grateful. When our perception of being harmed changes to one of being helped, our emotions shift. Our emotional reactions also influence intentional energy. Being passionate about something can intensify our desire for it; love or hate can fuel the pursuit of an interest. Emotions such as being fulfilled and appreciated may also influence our interests and desires. We may be more likely to want to contribute if we believe we will be appreciated. How we've felt in the past (our emotional memories) influences how we expect to feel in the future (our mental conclusion) and therefore influences what we decide to pursue (our intention).

The formative information in these three groups can intensify, complement, conflict with, or negate other formative information. Thus, our creative energy—our formative beliefs, feelings, and desires—can be out of balance, conflicted, and working against us, or it can be aligned, in balance, and focused on creating what we deeply want. How aligned and consistent our formative information is determines how successful we are in consciously attracting what we want. For example, if you intend to be in a loving relationship, but feel unlovable and don't believe you'll ever find love, your intentional energy conflicts with your emotional and mental energy. Because these energies are working against each other your desire is not fulfilled. Instead of finding a loving relationship you have the experience of "wanting," which creates loneliness rather than a loving relationship. However, we do attract what we want on some level—our unconscious desires, full of self-doubt, call for rejection from others because we want to confirm our view.

BECOMING AWARE OF HUMAN ENERGY FIELDS

Becoming aware of human energy fields can help us begin to understand our energy fields and the formative information at work within us. (Remember, formative information is the intentions, feeling, and beliefs each of us carries around, which are active in our energy fields.) Our emotions help us sense formative information in others. For example, we may notice when someone close to us is feeling tense, sad, or excited. We may be able to sense harmful intentions. We may know someone who has mood swings and ask if she is having a bad day. We may have a sense when it is safe to bring up touchy subjects. We may have made mistakes about someone's mood and learned to beware of her reactions. Children who grew up in abusive situations have a highly developed awareness of emotional/intentional energy (formative information) because their survival depends on knowing when to keep quiet or hide. We may not be consciously aware of someone else's field, but may suddenly find ourselves feeling tense or uncomfortable because of someone's emotional or intentional energy.

Did you ever have the experience of someone being attracted to you, and even though that person said nothing, you knew? Or you may notice tension in the way a married couple in your circle of friends is interacting with each other. Perhaps your normal way of relating goes haywire when you visit your relatives over the holidays. If these situations seem familiar, you have a healthy awareness of human energy fields.

Consciously or unconsciously perceiving someone else's energy field is like walking by a man smelling of fresh after-shave. When we are close to him, we are highly aware of the fragrance. Farther away, we are not as influenced by the smell. The stronger the fragrance, the more we are influenced. We detect scent with our sense of smell.

We perceive human energy fields with our intuition and all five senses—shaking or touching hands, seeing a wrinkled forehead or smile lines, smelling a pungent or sweet scent, tasting a kiss, hearing harshness or welcome in a voice. Most of us also have a sixth sense, a gut feeling, or an intuitive hit which picks up, sorts, and packages the tangible and intangible formative information we perceive about others. We notice and interpret this information with our thoughts, our emotions, and our desires. If we feel intimidated by someone and want to stay away from that person, we may be sensing and interpreting formative information from his energy field. Most of us feel comfortable and safe with some people, but wary of others. Our responses may come from past interactions or from something we sense without any previous contact. In the latter case, we are sensing and interpreting the person's energy field.

This is a two-way interaction. The effect of a person's energy field on you has to do with your own energy field. Someone you feel uncomfortable with might feel perfectly comfortable to someone else. It's the interaction of human energy fields that produces the reaction. For example, some of the same people who enjoyed my company also enjoyed the board president's company. However, we never felt comfortable with each other.

Once a friend and I left a downtown movie theater at dusk and walked toward my car. A man crossed the street in the middle of the block and headed straight for us. I felt anxious. Without speaking, my friend and I raced to my car. Driving away, locked inside the car, my friend and I confirmed our shared experience. Even though we had passed other street people outside the theater, none of them had set off warning signals in us as that man had. We both sensed a menacing intention.

I believe that animals can sense intentional and emotional energy. My friend Ann claims that when she is feeling ill, her cat sits in her lap or close to her, but when she is feeling frustrated or angry, her cat hides. Beekeepers know that approaching a beehive confidently has a calming effect on bees. Mail carriers and meter readers know the difference between encountering a dog with fear and with trust. Dogs seem to sense the difference immediately.

Animals and people who are sensitive to human energy can read our emotions and intentions. Sometimes others are more aware of the formative information in our energy fields than we are. Have you ever asked someone if he was angry and his response was "No! I'm not!" You had sensed something about that person's emotional energy that he was not conscious of. Chances are, later that person may realize that he was angry.

Our energy fields telecast information about us. We are aware of some of the messages we are transmitting and unaware of others.

When Energy Fields Meet

We are influenced by and influence other people's energy fields. For example, you may feel animated and excited as you encounter someone who is frustrated and upset. The emotional energy of each field has an effect on the other. As the formative information from the two fields merge, you may feel less exuberant, and the other person may feel less troubled. If the fields influence each other sufficiently, the two of you can interact comfortably, and the dissimilar energy fields will become a single, merged energy field. If the fields fail to come into balance, you or the other person may move away in attempt to protect the autonomy of your energy field.

Here is an illustration. A nurse sweeps into a patient's room, delivering a flood of cheerful comments while briskly performing her duties. The patient, slowed down by medication and pain, cringes and shrinks from her. The difference in energy level is grating to the patient unable to merge his energy with hers. The nurse, on the other hand, has to work hard keeping her energy up around depressed patients in pain. It is easier on everyone when nurses and other visitors enter a little more slowly and quietly, matching the energy of the patient. The energy fields merge more easily then.

A group of people can merge their energy fields so that they can work together more easily. Meetings at work often begin with social banter which allows the fields to merge. People can then interact more comfortably. A single person can shift the energy field of a group, as when a somber intruder enters a room where people are laughing. The laughter can die down quickly, but when the intruder leaves, the laughter may return. Giggling teenage girls, and their parents are familiar with this type of unbalanced energy field.

Energy Fields at Home

Have you noticed how hard it is to get the people in your family to change how they relate to each other? Perhaps your mom or dad is distant or unavailable, and you haven't been able to change them. Maybe you are the person your family is trying to change, and you may be resisting their suggestions. Carefully crafted, long-standing energy fields sustain family interaction patterns. Similar to inertia, these energy fields tend to resist change. One person with a good understanding of how energy fields work can change these family patterns, however.

For example, my friend Jenny worked on her beliefs and patterns (remember, each of us carries our beliefs and patterns in our energy field) for several years, and her relationship with her parents changed dramatically. She thought her parents had changed and become much more accepting and loving. Jenny told her sister that her visit home was much easier since they had undergone this transformation. Her sister, encouraged by the news, went home for a visit, but came back disheartened. She reported to Jenny that their parents had not changed. "In fact, they're worse than ever. They spent the whole weekend telling me how to run my life." Jenny had transformed her part of the family energy field, her interaction with her parents, but the traditional family energy field still existed for her sister.

Energy Fields at Work

Many corporations work to change their company "culture." Culture is a system of beliefs and actions that characterize a certain group. A culture is an energy field. Many efforts to change a culture fail, and it is common to hear people say, "The more things change the more they stay the same." Corporate culture energy fields are resistant to change because they are made up of so many individual energy fields.

The cartoon *Dilbert* recounts the strange drama of stagnant organizational energy fields. Part of the reason for *Dilbert's* popularity is that so many of us can relate to a dysfunctional workplace. What we may not realize is that the difficulty in changing a dysfunctional culture rests in the nature of an organization's energy field. The field, having reached equilibrium, can be as resistant to change as Cape Perpetua.

You can become aware of energy fields at work by noticing if there are people who seem intimidating. Notice if your energy changes as you enter the workplace. Do you close off part of your personality because it's not all right to be your whole self at work? These are normal responses to working energy fields.

HOW ONE PERSON'S ENERGY FIELD CAN CHANGE ANOTHER'S ENERGY FIELD

Many people don't realize how clearly they broadcast their emotions and intentions. Have you ever felt someone enter the room, even though you didn't hear or see him? If a normally happy friend is feeling grumpy but hides it, you might sense the change in her energy field. It is easier to notice when our friends' emotions and intentions change because we know how they usually react.

While I was out for an early morning run a few years ago, I saw a woman leaning against the back door of her car with the driver's door hanging open. Stopping to see if she needed help, I realized it was Helen, the wife of our city manager, who lived several blocks from my house. I barely recognized her. She seemed smaller and more fragile than I remembered. I had read in the newspaper that she was fighting cancer. She told me she had just returned from a swim and she was resting.

Despite Helen's obviously weakened condition, she gave me a big smile, and went on to praise the work we had been doing at the utility. I had not felt appreciated at work recently, so I soaked in her attention. She shared with me that she felt at peace with her life. It was clear that she was facing her death with deep faith. I yearned to trust and believe in life as she did. Helen's intention to appreciate others and her unshakable faith flooded our shared energy field. Five minutes of conversation with her filled me with a powerful sense of peace. I felt whole and valued, as though I had stepped into an invisible field of grace. In that moment, I felt my energy expand to a more loving and trusting level.

When I continued on my run, instead of thinking about my job as I usually did, I noticed how beautiful the flowers were and how grateful I was to be alive. When I read several weeks later that Helen had died, I felt a sense of loss and promised myself that I would never forget her gift.

ENERGY FIELDS AT OUR BEST

Most of us have times when we feel fully alive, whole, complete, and brimming with energy. We feel resourceful and accomplished. What we want comes easily, almost magically. Our words and our actions seem to flow effortlessly with perfect timing. We are in the flow of life, energized and nurtured by gratitude and acceptance. Our energy seems to overflow, energizing others. We have a healthy glow. People tell us we look great. At such times, we are fully engaged. We breathe easily with an inner sense of openness and trust. Everyone looks radiant. Colors seem brighter. The whole world seems vital and alive.

This sense of ourselves and the world can be fleeting—a momentary glimpse of what life could be. But these moments give us hope and promise that it is possible to live that way. What we are experiencing at those times is an energy field unrestricted by the limitations of black holes.

An expanded energy field gives us a sense of wide contentment, like the ocean—constant, deep, and abiding—a sense of joy carried on a current of trust and faith. This energy is not the staccato high that we get from winning the final point in a close basketball game or the euphoria that comes from besting the field at the finish line. This is the deep knowing that we are having a winning season, a winning life.

When we are in this expansive, loving energy, we are a delight to be with. We are grounded in reality, yet open for the next moment. We are aligned with and pursuing our highest purpose, yet we are just being ourselves. Though we may not have much experience with this loving energy, all of us have the capacity to live in this way.

Unfortunately, we have black holes and energy patterns that prevent us from living our lives at our best. However, we can learn to balance and free our energy fields to create more of what we really want in our lives. As you read on, you can learn how to recognize the patterns in your field and change them. You will find a way to be true to yourself so that you can avoid the limitations and blocks that reduce your creative energy. You will be introduced to practices that will help you focus your creative energy so that you can more easily attract the experiences and people you want in your life. You will also learn about the collective energy field and the magnetic influence we have on each other. As you learn more about black holes and energy fields you may naturally release some of your energy blocks. By exploring human energy fields, understanding how they function, and exposing the secrets they hold, you can more easily and consciously align your life with your soul's desires.

Chapter Two

Black Holes

························

When Barbara's youngest daughter finally told her that her marriage was on the rocks, Barbara wanted to do something, anything, but couldn't make a move. It really hurt her—she considered it a perfect match, and they had a child they both loved.

Barbara's older two daughters had gotten married, had children, and divorced. Now Molly was following in their footsteps. Barbara slumped in a chair and sobbed, "Why can't my daughters have a normal life? Why can't Molly and Russ just tell each other the truth? If they would really talk to each other, they could work it out. I have to get them to talk with each other. I can't let this marriage fall apart."

Though she realized that her daughter needed to make her own decisions, she felt compelled to write her a letter, telling her how to save the marriage and adding the news that she was coming to see them in order to help. When Molly received the letter, she called and asked her mother not to come, that she had to work it out with her husband their own way. But Barbara couldn't let go. She was stuck in a big black hole.

A black hole is a concentration of balled-up emotional energy of unconscious stories, fears, and beliefs. Black holes are triggered by outside events, such as Molly's divorce, but our reaction to these events comes from inside us, not outside us. How we react depends upon the emotional memories we have accumulated and the defenses that mask our black holes.

Like most of us, Barbara didn't realize she was in a black hole. She focused her energy—thought energy in the form of judgment, emotional energy in the form of agitation, and intention energy in the form of blame—on Molly. Blame and judgment are two of the masks for our black holes.

In the physical universe, along with energy fields, planets, solar systems, and galaxies, astronomers have identified phenomena called black holes. A black hole is a giant mass in space so dense that its gravitational force sucks in all particles and energy that come within its field. Black holes function like giant vacuum cleaners in space.

Just as giant black holes exist in the universal field of energy, we have our own black holes within our personal energy fields. I use the metaphor of a black hole because our beliefs and the stories that created them are missing from our consciousness as if they were sucked into a black hole. Our black holes function like mini vacuum cleaners, whisking painful experiences out of our awareness. However, black holes are a useful feature of human energy fields: if we were completely aware of all the disturbing things that have ever happened to us, we couldn't function. In that respect, our black holes help us function normally. When we are children and have scary experiences, we don't have the emotional maturity to deal with them. Even as adults, we can't always take the full force of an emotional trauma at the time it occurs. Our black holes store these experiences for us to deal with later. They suck up these memories, concealing them from us so that we can go on with our lives. We have conscious fragments of these emotional stories, but little access to how we felt and what we decided to believe as a result of what happened. As we grow older, our stash of painful, secret stories grows too.

While our black holes help us by protecting us from dealing with painful memories and troubling experiences, a down side is that they also disrupt our creative energy. The formative information in our black holes (the beliefs, feelings, and intentions that focus our creative energy) usually conflicts with our conscious intentions to be fulfilled and happy. When some experience brings back any memory that was hidden in our black holes, we emotionally re-experience that event as though it was happening now. We may not remember anything about the original event, but we still react emotionally and feel small, inadequate, helpless, and stuck. We may experience a flood of alarming emotions such as humiliation, jealousy, or terror.

In Barbara's case, behind her despair about her daughter Molly's separation, she discovered the following story hidden in her black hole. "My husband and I had been married for twenty-seven years when we separated and divorced. I went to visit my parents in another state, and for the first time in my life I said no to my father over a trivial matter. He looked at me and said angrily, 'You will never be happy, and I wish I had never given you a dime.' As I packed my bag and fled, I was shaking, afraid I was going to die. I went to a hotel and checked myself in, but couldn't sleep a wink. I didn't know what to do. I had no one to turn to. And I was still shaking."

Barbara buried this story in a black hole, along with her feelings of shame, terror, and humiliation. Her other two daughters were divorced from their husbands. And now when her last daughter, her youngest, joined her sisters, she absolutely couldn't stand by and do nothing. In actuality, she was trying to avoid the pain of her own divorce.

It wasn't until Molly's separation that Barbara found this story and several others that had prompted her hysterical reaction. As she released her black holes, as she grew aware of her response to her father and her own divorce, her anxiety about Molly diminished. She felt sad about the divorce, but no longer felt it necessary to intervene.

When we recreate a black hole experience, our perception of the world changes. It seems like a scarier, more hostile place. We can't remember what it was like to feel good about ourselves. The beliefs and emotions tucked in these stories unconsciously influence our behavior, and we may make mistakes in judgment that hurt important relationships. Barbara's interference strained her relationship with Molly at a time when her daughter simply needed her mother's support.

The following list suggests some of the emotional memories that may be stored in our black holes. See if any of these experiences are familiar.

- Having your parents separate or divorce
- Not feeling safe with your brother, mom, dad, or your mom's boyfriend
- Feeling lost, left out, or not wanted
- Not feeling trusted to do things for yourself
- Being chosen last
- Being teased or laughed at
- Having to take care of your mom or dad
- Having to fight to protect yourself
- Being subject to violence or a shocking scene
- Suffering from an accident or serious illness
- Moving a lot, having to start over
- Being threatened or beaten up by tougher kids
- Being singled out or humiliated
- Losing one or both parents, a brother, or a sister
- Being shuffled from one family to another, never having a real home

How you felt when these experiences happened and the beliefs you developed about yourself as a result are preserved in a black hole.

In addition to painful events in our childhood, disastrous historical events—the plague, the slaughter of native tribes, slavery, the Depression, the Holocaust, World War II, and the Vietnam War—leave archetypal memories in our collective human energy field. These stories affect some people more than others and accumulate in their black holes.

One way to recognize that you have a black hole is to notice a shift in your usual mood or behavior. If you are normally talkative and energetic, a black hole may render you depressed and quiet. If you are normally quiet and calm, you may suddenly lash out with a sarcastic or cynical remark. If you are normally analytical and unemotional, a black hole may trigger a flash of anger.

Hormonal fluctuations, as with premenstrual syndrome (PMS) or menopause, can result in black holes triggering more easily. Women with PMS may recognize an almost hair-trigger sensitivity once a month.

Once triggered, a black hole can quickly and unpredictably shift us into an altered emotional and mental state, much like turning Dr. Jekyll into Mr. Hyde. Yesterday we were fine; today we're defensive, scrambled, depressed, troubled, or we identify others as the problem. For example, if we think people have discounted us, we may blame them for our wounded feelings. We don't realize that they have triggered an old wound. If we hate our job, we may not realize that something about our job triggers unresolved emotional stories.

When a black hole has been triggered, we can feel swamped in emotional turmoil, lost in our own reaction. We may believe that there is no way out. If we do not understand that we are having a black hole experience, we are likely to feel like a victim and blame others for our reactions. If we have dozens of black holes (which is not uncommon), we have few resources, we can't be gracious to other people, we can't simply be interested in them, and no matter how much we receive from others, we have little to give back.

When I was in college, Trish, one of my roommates, wasn't sure what she wanted from life. In the years afterward, she usually called me when her job wasn't working out or when she had some problem she couldn't solve. Trish is smart and had a college degree, but she worked at meaningless jobs she didn't like. When she called, I would listen to her troubles, but no matter how much support I gave her, she continued to run into problems.

When Trish was in the grip of a black hole, she felt worthless, convinced she couldn't do anything right. Helpless and unable to change any situation, she believed that other people—her boss, her roommate, her family—were the source of her problems. Her energy drained away, and, hopeless, she sank continually into a depression that hung over her like a black cloud. Trish didn't realize she was protecting herself from the painful emotional stories hidden in her black holes.

If you're not aware of your black holes, think about a time when you told a highly opinionated person that he was wrong about something. He probably got steamed up trying to convince you he was right. This is how black holes work. The opinionated person was using his energy to keep from opening up the black hole where he stored the belief that he was not acceptable, or not good enough. He keeps on explaining how right he is in order to hide his own fears, and by being right, he tries to convince himself of his worthiness. "Accused" of not being right, his reaction takes on more bluster than is called for. He is masking his black hole by explaining his position in an attempt to hide his feelings of inadequacy—primarily from himself.

By their very nature, black hole experiences seem bigger than we are—more than we can handle. We can feel helpless and worthless. We can feel hopelessly caught in anxious disquiet. We can feel stuck and believe we have no choice in how to react. That is because we are reacting to our own painful emotional stories stored in our black holes.

TRIGGERS FOR BLACK HOLES

Triggers are words, actions, people, or situations that remind us of what is hidden in our black holes. Triggers are like hot buttons, or hooks. The black hole trigger in Barbara's case was her daughter's separation. When a black hole is triggered, our unconscious personal history is exposed. For example, being criticized may trigger an emotional memory. When someone suggests that we've done something wrong, or that someone has a problem with us and is avoiding us, this can trigger one of our black holes. We usually don't realize what is happening and react more strongly than the criticism or the problem warrants.

Black holes are more likely to trigger if our failure is pointed out in front of others, a double blow reawakening past humiliation in addition to hopelessness. Our faces might get red or we might feel a little sick inside. We might feel defensive or make excuses to keep from feeling the raw, disturbing emotions in our black holes. When we trip into the jumble of emotions below the surface, we may feel as if we were drowning, and as we work to stay above the surface of our own reactions, we use up energy treading emotional hot water.

We become lost in our reaction and have little energy left to handle the situation.

PROTECTIONS AND DEFENSES FOR BLACK HOLES

Given such reactions, it's natural that we would want to avoid whatever brings our black holes to life. Most people live much of their lives trying to avoid these triggers. Barbara did so by living hundreds of miles from her daughters, a common avoidance strategy.

There's a problem once someone triggers one of our black holes. We may become puzzled as to whether the problem is one of our black holes or simply an offensive person. In other words, is our reaction absurd because it is a reaction to a black hole, or is it justified? Figuring this out can make us feel crazy. The key is to notice our own reaction. If we have a reaction, we have a potential black hole.

We develop protections and defenses to keep our black holes from triggering, and to keep our reactions and the emotional stories connected with them securely hidden. We've stored difficult experiences and limiting beliefs in our black holes because we don't know how to deal with them. It is easier to deny our vulnerability, fears of inadequacy, and loss. In denial, we don't recognize or claim our black holes; instead, we protect ourselves with automatic behavior patterns that keep them in the dark, submerged. Denial doesn't change our black holes, it just allows us not to look at them.

As I mentioned earlier, one of the indicators that we have touched a black hole is overreacting to a situation, making a mountain out of a molehill. Have you noticed that you sometimes react more strongly than a present situation calls for? Your spouse reminds you to take out the garbage and you feel defensive. A co-worker gets promoted and you feel like a failure. Your best friend decides not to go on a trip with you and you feel betrayed. Someone tells you that you are wrong and you feel enraged. You make a small mistake and beat yourself up about it for days. We usually blame such reactions on someone else. Blaming helps us protect the real cause of our reaction, our own emotional stories.

Blame is the quickest and easiest way to cover a black hole. If we can find someone else to blame, we'll feel better almost immediately. As with other protective mechanisms, it doesn't accomplish much and is likely to prompt a defensive or blaming reaction from the other person. We may feel better, but nothing has been released or resolved.

Trying to get people to change is a similar strategy. For example, if you can trigger a black hole by ignoring me, then I will work hard to get you to pay attention to me. If I can get you to do so, I'll feel better. Another person might trigger a black hole by saying untrue things about me. If I become enraged and call him a "liar," I am reacting to my own black hole—my fear that what he's said will hurt me or is partially true. Training all the people who might trigger my black holes is a big undertaking. There are so many people to train.

Distraction is another common defense. For example, if one of my black holes is triggered, I may choose to read a book, watch TV, or go to the movies rather than wallow in my feelings. By expanding my focus to other experiences, my black hole takes a back seat in my conscious attention. Distractions are preferable to obsessing. The persistent use of distractions, however, can leave us confused, exhausted, or addicted. Addictions to alcohol, drugs, TV viewing, gambling, shopping, overeating, or working long hours are common distractions for our black holes. Many war veterans have developed addictions to fight off war memories that threaten to erupt into their conscious awareness. Used habitually, distractions obscure our black holes so that we don't search for the source of our reaction and release it.

As another defense, we may try to fix the lives of our friends and family. Serving people we care about is a worthy activity and a way to grow beyond black holes, but we can also use it to mask our black holes. We may keep them from being triggered by unconsciously pirating energy from the people we believe need help. For example, social service agencies usually have one or more employees who look down on clients as a way to feel better about themselves and deny that they have black holes. If we instead put our helping energy into releasing our black holes and accepting ourselves as we are, we can ultimately be of greater service to others.

Some people have a pattern of hating or raging at others when they feel vulnerable and scared. Rage is a desperate attempt to keep vulnerable emotions hidden. Hate separates us from our reaction by placing blame on an identifiable individual or group. Both of these reactions are an unconscious attempt to mask our black holes and quiet our secret emotional stories. Unfortunately, these masks stir up more problems for us than we already have tucked away in our black holes.

See if you recognize the following masks and defenses used to cover black holes: avoiding others, blaming others, critical judgment, rage, hate, confusion, addictions, complaints, defensiveness, explanations of rightness, hyperactivity, busyness, superiority, distractions, denial.

We all have our own ways of keeping the contents of our black holes a secret from others and ourselves. Some of us need to be right all the time. Others pretend they are better than others. Busyness, blame, confusion, and other strategies on the list keep us from fully experiencing our black holes. These strategies convince us that our problems exist out there beyond our energy fields. Our masks and defenses allow us to give up responsibility for our actions. We give control of our lives to external forces, triggers, and events. However, despite our maneuvers, most of us experience a black hole from time to time, if not daily

BLACK HOLES AND FALSE BELIEFS

Black holes hide our limiting and negative beliefs about ourselves. These are part of the formative information that empowers our creative energy. Since beliefs have been remembered and retraced many times, they are more potent than fleeting thoughts. Conscious awareness is not necessary for our beliefs to exert their influence. If we believe we are attractive, we are. If we believe we are not attractive, we aren't. If we believe that we are not very intelligent, we will notice normal forgetfulness and retrace the belief. If we believe that we are intelligent, we will excuse forgetfulness as a momentary lapse rather than a sign of deficient mental powers.

Keen or quick understanding of a subject will serve as proof, increasing the creative energy of the belief.

At the core of every black hole are disturbing emotions such as fear or humiliation, accompanied by one or more unconscious limiting beliefs. These beliefs seem like the truth when they are not. In eighth grade, our teacher asked us to prepare an impromptu speech about an article in *Time* magazine. I was assigned an article about that week's stock prices. I read and reread the article for the full five minutes we were given to prepare, but didn't understand it. When I got up to speak, I felt panicky and hopelessly lost. For years, the humiliation I felt that day resurfaced every time I was asked to speak in front of a group (although I didn't connect it to my eighth-grade trauma). By reliving that experience again and again in my mind I developed a belief that I wasn't a good speaker.

Like me, you may believe that you are inadequate or unacceptable in some way—not competent to do something right or not resourceful enough to get what you want. You may have a belief that you are unattractive or unlovable. These beliefs seem true based on the experiences stored in your black holes. Defensive patterns surface when situations or people remind us of our limiting beliefs. I protected myself for years by declining speaking invitations or anxiously overpreparing.

Although we use many different defensive patterns to hide our black holes, we all share the basic emotions and beliefs stored in those holes. There are four basic false, limiting beliefs: not capable, not lovable, not resourceful, and not empowered.

The not capable belief is that we are incompetent. We believe that we are not smart enough, not strong enough, not healthy enough, not organized enough, not knowledgeable, not educated, not competent. Our primary fear is of failure. This belief is more than healthy self-questioning. It is debilitating, immobilizing self-doubt. We may feel overwhelmed with fear, terrified to venture beyond our known patterns and territory. From a black hole containing this belief, it is hard to take action that tests our capability.

The not lovable belief is based on a sense of unworthiness. We believe that we are not worthy of love and acceptance, not attractive enough, not nice enough, not acceptable in some way. We believe that we don't deserve love and affection. We feel vulnerable, unlovable, abandoned, or rejected. Our black hole may contain a belief that we are a "bad" person or have done unforgivable things, and therefore cannot be included, forgiven, appreciated, or loved. In the extreme, the belief is a form of self-hate with feelings of despair and separation from others.

The not resourceful belief is that we cannot create what we want in life. We can't attract the jobs, the people, or the financial resources we want. It is based on a belief that there is not enough to go around and we are one of the have-nots. It is a belief that we don't deserve the good things life has to offer. We are not entitled to have a full, rich life. We believe in scarcity rather than abundance. We may be afraid that we will never be able to replace a lost love. A black hole containing this belief is filled with anger, regret, and sadness that we can't have what we want. There may be a significant amount of blame that lives here. We may believe that others are responsible for our present, unsatisfactory lives.

The not empowered belief insists that we try to please others. We may feel hopeless without their approval. We may yearn for acknowledgment and recognition. We may believe that we are not enough on our own, that we can't stand alone, that we can't trust ourselves or the world around us. Fear is our primary experience. We are afraid that others won't like us, or approve of us, or won't accept us. We don't feel safe. We think that safety comes from others. This false belief convinces us to look to others to decide what to do, what to say, and how to look. It is denial of self at a core level. There is usually much sadness around our decision not to be who we really are. It is the betrayal of self that fills this black hole with such grief.

BLACK HOLES LIMIT HEALTHY EMOTIONS

When we are unfettered by black holes, healthy human emotions flow freely. If our formative information is balanced and aligned, we experience an ebb and flow of our emotions. We don't get stuck in any one emotional experience. Uncomfortable feelings such as hopelessness and rage are transient, just like happiness. When our energy is balanced, we accept our fear and sadness in the same way that we accept our joy and gratitude—with curiosity and wonder. Emotions that we accept will flow and change naturally, and become useful information for healthy living.

Most of us, however, have at least some of our healthy emotions sequestered in black holes. Perhaps exuberance wasn't acceptable at home and we were told to put it under wraps. And we acquiesced by putting that exuberance in a black hole along with the interaction that convinced us to put it there. Or our experiences with anger may have persuaded us to hide that emotion in a black hole.

When we limit the range of acceptable emotions, we may appear to be even-tempered, but there will be occasions when something triggers an emotional reaction that bulges out of our limited range. We may blow up, feel depressed, or have secret addictions—all bulges unacceptable to us. These emotional bulges suggest that black holes are hiding some of our healthy emotions, limiting them in unhealthy ways.

The reason we've been encouraged to hide our emotions is to restrain the behaviors we associate with these emotions. For example, anger is associated with loud voices and physical violence. Sorrow is associated with crying and acting helpless. You probably associate certain behaviors with each of the emotions in the list below. These associations are strong. Many people don't know how to feel an emotion without acting it out. Not having developed emotional intelligence, we seek instead to limit our range of experience.

Unfortunately, limiting emotions is not effective. It's like squeezing a half-filled balloon to make it smaller. The air must go somewhere and will pop out unexpectedly between your fingers. People who are emotionally restricted usually experience emotional bulges or spikes, with the suppressed terror or grief popping out in depression or an angry blow-up. After blowing up, they return to their limited emotional range. Anger, blame, and judgment are sometimes used to protect deeper, more painful emotions. Road rage and shooting rampages are examples of extreme emotional bulges or spikes.

A Healthy Range of Human Emotions

1.	excited, loving, joyful, happy, grateful, creative, passionate, compassionate, exuberant
2.	pleased, kind, hopeful, curious, patient, satisfied, generous, content, appreciative
3.	fine, cynical, OK, numb, bored, comfortable, depressed, uncomfortable
4.	anxious, afraid, angry, sad, envious, restless, frustrated, impatient, vulnerable
5.	hostile, terrified, enraged, grieving, hateful, jealous, devastated, disgusted, humiliated

Most people are comfortable along line 3. When someone asks us how we are, we often answer with terms from this line, "fine" or "OK." We tend to believe that this line is the most acceptable.

Many people allow themselves the middle three horizontal lines of emotions, 2,3, and 4, but they may not speak about these emotions or claim them outright. I have found that few people allow themselves the full range of emotions. Fewer still allow themselves to feel line 1 and line 5 with equal acceptance. By acceptance, I mean allowing ourselves to simply experience these emotions without acting out or behaving differently—without protecting, defending, or judging ourselves for feeling them.

When we allow our emotions to be fully present, they move and change from one moment to the next. When we experience what is stored in one of our black holes—feeling anxious, scrambled, or struggling—but don't allow ourselves the full experience, we can get emotionally stuck. Many people who suffer depression are in such a situation. When they experience the edge of a black hole—feeling down and anxious—they can't pull themselves out of it and are unwilling to experience what is hidden deeper in the hole.

If we allow ourselves to experience our natural emotions, we don't have to stay emotionally stuck. Allowing ourselves to understand and experience our hidden story can release stuck emotions and allow them to flow freely again. For instance, instead of staying stuck in the experience of anxiousness when I'm asked to speak now, I found and re-experienced the story of myself in eighth grade. Now I allow myself to feel the fear and the joy of speaking to groups. I don't think we can eliminate our emotions, but staying stuck isn't the answer. Allowing our emotions to flow releases our formative information and gives us a chance to align and consciously direct our creative energy.

Moreover, when we do so, we feel fully alive. Unless we allow ourselves to grieve deeply, we will not experience our gratitude. The same black holes where we experience our pain and our sorrow is where we store our joy. In trying to avoid line 5 on the emotional chart, we lose the top of our emotional range. If we expand our emotional range to include fear, we will also find our excitement. The top and bottom of the range expand together.

Most of us have found a safe, limited way to experience the ends of our emotional spectrum. For example, sporting events allow us to feel excited and humiliated. Television and movie actors and actresses portray emotions that trigger our own emotions.

Western culture values emotional control. When we feel exuberant, we may feel obligated to tone down our joy. If we are grieving the loss of someone close to us, we may keep our sorrow to ourselves or feel the need to apologize for it. People who don't allow themselves a full range of emotional expression are more comfortable when others limit themselves similarly. People with black holes usually hide their most joyous and most painful emotions. When others display these emotions, it taps at the door of their black holes and threatens to trigger hidden emotional memories.

To be fully human is to experience a full range of emotion. When we open ourselves to the flow of human emotions, we expand our creative energy. Our emotional experiences change moment by moment, flowing like a river, sometimes moving slow and deep, sometimes rushing in a waterfall of excitement. Black holes, on the other hand, are emotionally stagnant holding tanks. Without a flow of fresh water, life suffocates. Similarly, black holes choke off the flow of creative life-giving energy. They are like unhealthy septic tanks, building the gasses that pressurize our lives.

Emotional intensity popping out to relieve any pressure indicates a black hole. We can use this emotional intensity to find and release our black holes. By doing so, we increase our range of emotion and our awareness of our patterns and motivations. Acceptance of our emotional experiences allows our feelings to ebb and flow naturally. As we release our emotional memories, we restore a healthy flow of emotional energy. Expanding our conscious emotional range aligns our formative information and creative power. Free-flowing emotional energy gives us more conscious creative energy. We are able to attract more of what we want in our lives.

Many of us would prefer to think that bad things simply happen to us, that we are victims. Yet we know that two people growing up in similar situations can live very different lives. Some of us overcome dysfunctional environments to become fulfilled, contributing members of society. Others from the same family or neighborhood become victims or perpetrators. Some of the youngsters who have turned guns on their schoolmates are from homes with material advantages. While there are many other factors at work, I believe that people who live healthy, fulfilled lives have less of their creative energy hidden in unconscious black holes.

Unfortunately, many people would rather face actual physical harm or serious illness than encounter their own inner emotional stories directly. In the face of physical threat, we can rely on action. We can flee or fight, or throw ourselves at the feet of medical science. We have adrenaline to kick us into gear. But when we experience our own black holes, we must face what scares us most and our own worst beliefs about ourselves.

Fortunately, we can free our stories, beliefs, and expectations from our black holes. We can bring them into our conscious awareness and release them, so that they will no longer determine how we behave and react. When we release these emotional stories and change our beliefs, we shift from manifesting unconscious emotions and beliefs to consciously creating what we want most deeply.

Our willingness to allow ourselves to experience our pain and fear is what strengthens our soul. If an experience didn't trouble or terrify us, we wouldn't have hidden it away. By facing the worst, we build our inner strength to face future physical and emotional challenges. When we notice our pain, who is it that notices? When we acknowledge our fear, who is it that acknowledges? When we face ourselves, who faces us? Where is our awareness? I believe that the observer who acknowledges and notices is our soul. By reflecting on our thoughts and emotions, we energize and strengthen our spiritual essence—our soul. In releasing our black holes, we give our souls a workout and free our creative energy to create the lives we truly want more consciously. Balanced, aligned spiritual energy is the life force that enables us to live a fulfilled life.

Chapter Three

Energy Pirating and Black Holes

························

When I started working for the electric utility, I had to attend an executive staff meeting. The senior managers sat in plush swivel chairs around a long, polished oak table. Daylight filled the room from the glass north wall. Trusted managers with higher status sat closer to Keith, the chief executive. Those of us who played bit parts sat stiffly in straight-back chairs along the wall.

The agenda that day was personnel policy recommendations. Norm, the director of administration, reviewed the policy changes. One of his suggestions was that people be given the opportunity to form committees to advise the chief executive on issues that would directly affect their work.

When Norm mentioned the word "committees," Keith's face started turning red, and when Norm finished, all eyes swiveled to Keith, whose face matched his bright red tie. He stared at Norm for a moment, "What kind of a recommendation is employee committees? All committees ever do is take up time so nobody gets any work done. Norm, don't go fiddling around in other people's business. The whole company would be better off without your ideas." Everyone in the room sat perfectly still, barely breathing.

Herb, the director of operations, broke the silence. "I agree with Keith. Committees probably aren't a very good idea." Everyone at the table quickly agreed to delete the suggestion from the report. The meeting continued as normal, though Norm didn't say much.

When we come together, human energy is freely exchanged in

the form of compliments, gifts, money, attention, and friendship. When we love and believe in a child, we give him or her energy. When energy fields balance and merge, energy flows freely back and forth in personal relationships. Many relationships are not balanced, however. There are people, like Keith, who demand our agreement, attention, and support. When they do so, they are attempting to pirate our energy to feed their own. Even though we may feel wary or reluctant, we often give them what they want— just as all the people at the meeting gave Keith what he wanted. When we do this, we are allowing our energy to be pirated.

We give up energy this way because of our black holes. We are afraid we'll lose a relationship, approval, a job, or be blamed or harmed in some way. These fears of loss are hidden in our black holes. Anyone who triggers our black holes can successfully pirate our energy. They aren't pirates in the historical sense, plundering at knifepoint. They are simply seeking to meet their need, sometimes through force, and our black holes may lead us to think we have no choice but to go along. I believe that most of us, like Chief Executive Keith, are capable of slipping into unconscious energy pirate patterns to get our energy needs met.

People engaged in energy pirating get us to cater to them, accommodate them, follow their rules, or spend our energy supporting them in some way, perhaps as simply not voicing our opinions or asking for what we want. Or we may choose our words carefully. Or we may get drawn into others people's projects or even plan projects for them, when we'd rather not. Or we may pour our energy into guiding or helping others. We may change our behavior when we feel threatened by our family members, co-workers, neighbors, boss, or groups in our community. In all these draining experiences I have described, we have allowed our energy to be pirated.

In giving in to pirate patterns, we give up some of who we are and what we want, but usually for good reason—we feel afraid or guilty. We don't want to risk losing love, losing face, losing position, or facing physical harm. These consequences seem worse than giving up what we want in order to accommodate and support others. These fears, the fears of guilt and loss, live in our black holes. Since we generally prefer to avoid the triggers that awaken our black holes, we often grant energy pirates what they seek. These pirate patterns are often quite subtle. We may think that we are going along because it is easier. Whatever our reasons, using our energy—our actions, our words, our resources—to help someone else deny her black holes (her own fears) drains our energy.

Pirate patterns are usually learned early in life. Most families have formed stable energy fields based on energy pirate patterns. A child's survival requires human energy in the form of nurturing and physical care. As children grow, they continue to need love and attention. In most families, children learn to attract the energy and resources they need to survive and thrive. They learn the family pirate patterns. Here is an example of how family interactions help develop energy pirate patterns. Johnny shuffles into the kitchen in baggy shorts and a T-shirt. Seeing his mom on the phone, he goes over to his sister Suzy, who is drawing at the counter, and yanks her ponytail. Suzy yells, "Stop that." Mom, the kitchen phone to her ear, says nothing. Johnny, wanting attention, does it again. Suzy slams her magic marker down and yells for him to stop. Mom puts her hand over the phone and says, "Kids, I'm on the phone." Suzy protests, "It's Johnny's fault—he's pulling my hair with his dirty hands." Mom finally says, "Johnny, stop that."

Johnny has learned that when he wants attention, a form of energy, all he has to do is cause trouble. Suzy waits until her mom is off the phone and then presents her drawing inscribed, "To Mom with Love." Suzy seeks energy in the form of approval. Johnny and Suzy have different pirate patterns or strategies to get the energy they need to thrive. Johnny causes trouble. If Johnny doesn't get noticed, he escalates his behavior until he gets the attention he is after. He is developing a pattern of being difficult in order to get the energy he needs. Eager for praise, Suzy knows that if she does the right thing she will get the approval and recognition energy she needs. These are two common energy-pirating patterns at work in families.

We get energy from each other. We experience this energy when we feel a little better about ourselves, stand a little taller, and have more energy to think, speak, or act. Attention and love is energy. Put yourself in the following situations and imagine receiving attention and love energy:

- Co-workers celebrate your accomplishments.
- You are recognized and introduced at an awards dinner.
- Your parents tell you they are proud of your work.
- People at work come to you for advice or answers.
- The boss listens carefully to what you are saying.
- A neighbor tells you she appreciates being able to count on you.
- A friend says you look great.

Even one person can give you energy by joking with you or paying attention to you. Having several people pay attention to you gathers more energy. Think about a time when you were asked to say a few words to a group, large or small. At first you may have felt nervous, but afterward you were energized. The rush of energy that accompanies the audience's attention is familiar to every actor and public speaker. It is part of the lure of the stage.

The attention, approval, acceptance, love, support, comfort, acknowledgment, and recognition energy come from others. The process of gaining attention can be socially acceptable: being kind to someone, being right, being the boss, getting promoted, completing a project, cooking a great dinner, making a speech, running for office, or becoming a sports or television personality. However, attention can also be gained through socially unacceptable behavior: violence, shouting, or rudeness. Being the focus of attention normally is energizing even when the attention is harsh.

Not everyone wants attention energy all the time. There are times when we want to be left alone to recharge our energy. When we have black holes and live with people who are energy pirates, we may have more energy when we are alone, but almost all of us feel more energy when someone understands us, or encourages us. On the flip side, getting other people to do what we want gives us energy. When things go our way, we feel empowered. If we have political objectives, financial goals, or career aspirations—when we seek and get votes, sales, or promotions, we are energized. Other people are giving us what we want—money, presents, agreement. Think about when you got something you were hoping for. Remember how you felt then—excited, pleased, energized.

In healthy relationships, there is a normal give and take of energy. Energy pirates don't realize they are taking our energy, so it's mostly take and little give. People pirating energy require energy from others because of their black holes that continually need protection from being triggered.

In Chief Executive Keith's case, he demanded agreement energy from his managers perhaps because he felt inadequate or was afraid of failure and believed he would lose control of the company if employees were allowed input. Keith controlled his fear by intimidating others so that they agreed with him. Keith could then avoid having his black holes triggered and having to face his hidden fears. His energy pirating had a serious, unintended consequence though—it kept new ideas to a minimum. After witnessing Keith's outbursts, his managers were reluctant to bring forward their ideas. The most successful companies need new ideas to develop improved products and services.

When we give in to energy pirates, it's a little like filling a leaky cup, with us as the faucet. By giving in to someone's demand for support, attention, or agreement, we escape triggering our own black holes and facing our fears, hidden vulnerabilities, and limiting beliefs. If we didn't have black holes to deny, we wouldn't feel compelled to give in. The managers were afraid of Keith's anger. They didn't want to experience failure or humiliation in front of others, so they publicly agreed with him. Their fears of failure and humiliation were stored in their black holes. In private, these managers had ideas they didn't voice in Keith's presence. When facing Keith, they agreed and supported his energy-pirating pattern.

Both the person pirating and the person giving up energy have black holes. People who pirate energy from others are also vulnerable to pirating. In fact, when we give in to pirating, we may be tempted to use our own pirate patterns to replace what is lost. This is not the easy give and take of balanced energy fields. Pirating is a lose-lose game. We give up energy and then turn to pirate others. Others give up energy and then pirate us in a desperate cycle. Whether our interactions are pirate patterns or healthy give and take depends on whether they are compulsively driven by black holes—all pirating patterns exist to keep the contents of black holes in the dark, hidden.

There are many ways to pirate energy. Some pirate patterns gain support and approval. Other pirate patterns seek confirmation and certainty. Some people use pirating for love and acceptance, while others want to be seen as correct or virtuous. Still others gain energy by being of service to others.

Energy pirate patterns fall into five basic categories. In this section, I describe each category and give an example of the pirate pattern involved. For fairness in language, I alternate use of the pronouns he and she with each pattern. My choice of pronouns has nothing to do with male or female energy patterns. Both men and women use all five pirate patterns.

I developed the structure of these patterns from the Enneagram. Developed in the ancient Sufi religious tradition, the Enneagram is a guide to personality types for the purpose of spiritual development. More recently, many individuals and groups have used the Enneagram as a tool for personal growth. For example, the Enneagram has been used in the Catholic Church's marriage encounter program to help couples understand each other better. Some corporate training specialists have discovered the Enneagram and are using it in employee development programs and team building.

There are nine Enneagram types designated by number: 1) the perfectionist, 2) the giver, 3) the performer, 4) the romantic, 5) the observer, 6) the skeptic, 7) the epicure, 8) the boss, and 9) the mediator. Each Enneagram type has a core fear: fear of being bad, needy, a failure, defective, insufficient, humiliated, not enough, powerless, having no heart.

I have identified five pirate patterns that combine the similar energy strategy characteristics of the nine Enneagram types and their core fears. People engaged in energy pirating usually practice more than one of these five pirate patterns or strategies. They may use one strategy with you and another one with me. You may recognize some of these energy strategies from your family, your workplace, or friends. The pirate patterns that show up in your life may be a combination of or a variation on these patterns. Most people use one pirate pattern more often, but not in all situations. People set a pirate pattern into motion when a situation threatens to expose their vulnerable emotions and limiting beliefs.

Pirate patterns seek a combination of power, love, and support. People playing pirate games want enough power to live their lives as they desire. They want to be accepted and loved for who they are, and they want the comfort of knowing that they're capable and sane. Pirating strategies have a positive intention, but pirating behaviors are counterproductive.

These five categories of pirate patterns provide a basic guideline to the behavior—it's not a detailed listing. My hope is that these five, along with the motivations for the behaviors, will begin to explain some of the experiences you may have had that seemed to drain your energy

The *Intimidator/Self-Righteous Energy Pirate* judges people, dismisses others, determines right and wrong, and demands that other people follow his rules. He wants respect and desires to be seen as correct and virtuous. This gives him a sense of power and security. He covers his fear with anger.

The *Victim/Anxious Energy Pirate* finds fault, bemoans the past, and worries about the future. She hopes to get help, sympathy, love, and approval to reduce her anxiety, and to feel safe and sane. She hides her fear with her helplessness.

The *Charmer/Trickster Energy Pirate* seeks to win favors, love, and approval by offering false support and attention with strings attached. He masks his fear by being charming or tricking others into giving him what he wants.

The *Performer/Comedian Energy Pirate* seeks recognition and attention in order to feel loved. She impresses others with her intelligence, capability, bold actions, or humorous comments. She hides her fear by seeking attention.

The Distant/Indifferent Energy Pirate attracts the concern and interest of others by keeping his distance and putting on a show of not caring. He wants people to seek him out, and regards their doing so as reassurance that he is capable, accepted, and sane. He calms his fears of being controlled by being distant.

INTIMIDATOR/SELF-RIGHTEOUS ENERGY PIRATE PATTERN

Intimidator pirate patterns are common in the workplace, especially in the executive suite. Chief Executive Keith played the role of an intimidator pirate. Intimidator pirating turned out to be common practice at that company. One day I suggested a new approach for public involvement to Herb, one of the directors at the utility. I suggested that we present alternative routes for a new transmission line to the public, along with advantages and disadvantages of each, so they would have an opportunity to comment. Herb's reaction was uncharacteristically intense. "Don't come back into operations if you're going to make lousy suggestions like that."

I felt attacked and scared. In retrospect, I believe that Herb felt threatened by my suggestion to involve the public in decisions that had formerly been his domain. The perceived threat triggered a black hole in which he may have felt afraid of losing full control. He covered it with an intimidator pirate pattern. One of my black holes triggered immediately. I was afraid of angry confrontations, so I gave him what he wanted. I dropped the idea. When we are confronted by intimidator pirating, we are likely to apologize, appease, and give in to them, as I did with Herb, and as the managers did with Keith.

A person using the intimidator pirate pattern works hard to do things correctly. He tends to see things in black and white and has a clear sense of what to him is right and wrong. Someone using this pattern has extensive analysis and moral justification for why the rules he follows are correct. If we do not follow the same rules, he can feel threatened and become irritated with us for not respecting the rules—his rules. He may feel resentful or resort to revenge as a way to have his energy needs met.

Being hard-wired for survival, in a tough situation he is capable only of a fight-or-flight response. Someone playing intimidator pirate will react in one of these two survival patterns—and is usually a master of both. He may withdraw from an uncomfortable situation in disgust, or fight for what he wants. Usually his attacks seem illogical: he may yell at someone to get security and acceptance, or he may be sarcastic so that he feels included and respected. He may get angry to get what he wants. Anger comes from his fear that he hasn't gotten or won't get what he wants, expects to get, or believes should be his.

Someone playing the intimidator energy pirate may question us and want us to be more responsive, or may believe that he knows what we should do and give us advice without being asked. He feels certain that he is right. He doesn't recognize that there are lots of right ways to do things. Teenage children often trigger their parent's self-righteous pirate patterns.

The false belief that affects him most is that he cannot get what he wants in life. He fears he is not resourceful or powerful. He needs to control situations in order to meet the high standards he has set for himself. He needs to convince others that he is morally correct. By assuming authority and trying to control his situation, he develops a false sense of safety. He reinforces his control with standards and morale correctness. These reinforcements form a fortress around his black holes so that he can deny his fears, and the scarcity beliefs he has hidden away.

The typical righteous pirate approach is to demand that we change. When we give up what we want and comply with the intimidating person's demands, our efforts protect him. If we accommodate him, it is easier for him—he expends less energy. If our behavior bothers him and he gets us to change, he gets to be right. He feels relieved and better about himself, and his vulnerabilities and limiting beliefs remain safely locked in his black holes. If his authority and rules are respected, he brings a great deal of energy and enthusiasm to his work and his family. If they are not respected, he runs the intimidator pirate strategy to regain control.

VICTIM/ANXIOUS ENERGY PIRATE PATTERN

A person using the victim/anxious energy pirate pattern wants to reduce her anxiety by feeling safe and accepted. She wants things to go well, to feel sane, secure, and loved. However, she doubts that she'll ever get what she wants. She can feel afraid to the point of paranoia. She assumes the worst, and complains about her health, her lack of money, and her troubles. She uses the victim pirate pattern to gain attention and sympathy energy. She needs the concern of others to soothe her deep anxiety. However, she can never feed her anxiety enough to eliminate the gnawing discomfort of her black hole. Here's an example.

Sally's mom called the third time that day, "You didn't call me back." "Mom, I haven't had time to get to the drugstore yet."

"I'm feeling worse and I thought you were going to get me something for the pain." "Mom, I am, but I just got home from work."

"That's all right. I've been in pain for a long time. It'll wait. My Social Security check should be here any day now. I don't really need much to eat anyway." "Mom, I'm going to get you something. I just need a little time."

"You take your time. I'll probably still be here."

Someone who plays the victim pirate is afraid she is helpless and worthless. She believes there is some serious flaw that makes her crazy and unlovable. She believes that she will never be able to get the things she wants in life. She craves acceptance and special treatment, but assumes that she will never get these things. These fears and beliefs live in her black holes, but are too terrifying to experience, so they influence her behavior on a subconscious level. The defeatist attitude is part of what hooks us into sympathizing and offering support for someone caught in the victim/anxious pirate pattern. Here are some other examples of this pattern. Someone who complains about everything. Someone who is always "down on his luck." Someone who finds fault with other people at work and believes that other people are the problem. Someone who sees catastrophes everywhere. "Nothing will ever turn out right." "Other people will get all the good jobs." "I'll probably get some horrible disease and be incapacitated and miserable."

Victim pirating can be very subtle. We all do it. Have you ever complained about not being recognized or given credit or said to someone, "I don't feel attractive," or "I'm not very good at this," in the hope that she will argue with you and reassure you? Do you infer bad intentions when someone confronts you or complains about you? Do you assume that someone, other than you, needs to change in order for you to feel better—someone at work, your boss, your spouse, your parents? If so, you are familiar with the victim/anxious pirate pattern.

This person usually identifies with the underdog. She may rebel against authority and gather allies in an us versus them standoff. Victim/anxious pirate patterns cultivate agreement on whom to blame for any problem. In most workplaces, there is a group of people playing victim pirate. For example, an anxious co-worker who complains about the boss to gain agreement and support from others is playing victim pirate. Victim pirating groups may blame management for problems at work, or one group may agree that another group is the problem. Victim pirating groups gather to complain and blame others. They mask their black holes by gaining a little security and acceptance from these blaming collectives. In his book *The Celestine Vision*, James Redfield identifies five control dramas, which describe what he calls "energy vampires." Though based on a different system, several of his control dramas are similar to the energy pirate patterns I have identified. Redfield calls the victim/anxious pirate pattern the "Poor Me" control drama. As he explains it, "The obvious strategy in the Poor Me drama is to throw us off balance and win our energy by creating a feeling of guilt or doubt on our part."

Our guilt or self-doubt can lead us to listen and sympathize with such "poor" persons. They may ask for our help and if we feel guilty enough we may help them and lend our energy to their predicament. More likely we will feel uncomfortable with their thirst for attention and want to distance ourselves from them. Whether we distance ourselves from them or help them, we are spending our energy dealing with the victim pirate pattern.

People in difficult circumstances, but not playing victim pirate, will talk about their situations and will take responsibility for their lives and decide what to do, or they will ask for help and then resolve the situation on their own. The person playing victim leaves what to do hanging in the air for us to deal with. They are hoping we will feel sorry for them and help out. Whenever you are moved to help someone because you feel guilty, check to see if you are dealing with a victim pirate pattern.

Charmer/Trickster Energy Pirate Pattern

The charmer/trickster energy pirate pattern seeks love, approval, and power. The charmer feels good about supporting us because he believes that we will give him what he wants. A person using this pattern gives us what we want in exchange for our approval, appreciation, agreement, acceptance, and willingness to give him what he wants. The charmer needs favors, which represent power and love to him. The trickster also wants favors, but has power confused with love. He appears to be charming at first in order to trick us into giving him the power, money, or sexual favors he wants.

Connie thought she had found the perfect mate. Robert seemed to adore her. He supported her in every way. He helped her with her work. He encouraged her and believed in her. Robert seemed happy to go to any restaurant or movie Connie suggested. She found him unusually easy to get along with. Connie didn't realize that Robert was accommodating her. She thought they both wanted the same things. Later, Robert complained to Connie that he was unhappy with their relationship. He said he wasn't getting his needs met. Confused, Connie asked what she should do differently. Robert said he wanted her to appreciate and support him the same way he did for her. Connie didn't know what to do.

From her perspective, everything was going well. In fact, Robert was playing the charming pirate, but wasn't getting what he wanted. Eventually, he found someone else to accommodate, and Connie was confused and heartbroken.

The charmer pirate pattern can be subtle. Someone engaging in this pattern can appear to be helpful. Support staff such as secretaries and office assistants are in a perfect position to be charming. A staff member who knocks himself out for the boss—puts the job ahead of his own needs—is seeking a reward. He has a way of letting others know how difficult his work is and how much effort he puts into satisfying their demands. He is seeking acknowledgment and appreciation.

Someone using the charming pirate pattern invests energy—he compliments, appreciates, gives in, helps, acts nice—to earn power. If he works hard to support others but gains little in return, he can feel cheated and resentful. Like investing in a company that fails, he may lose his initial energy capital. At that point, he may withdraw from the relationship, invest more energy hoping for a future payoff, or try a different pirate pattern.

The charming approach can feel energizing to the person he is with because his attention and flattery is enjoyable. But his desire for approval is high. If the next person after Connie doesn't give him back what he wants, there will be a change in strategy. His giving comes with strings attached. The problem appears when he doesn't receive the support or acknowledgment he expected in return. Giving is not the end he seeks. He craves to live as he chooses, but he is compelled to give to others because he doesn't feel powerful, needed, or appreciated. As long as he maintains his black holes, his charm will have strings attached.

A charming person wants us to like him. He will agree to do things he would rather not do in the hopes of getting back what he wants. If we refuse the deal, there is a withdrawal of affection. The trickster pattern is a more desperate version of charming. Bait and switch is part of the trickster pattern. Those who use the trickster pattern find people who are needy and promise to help them in some way. This help sounds good, but it is not. It is a way to access what the trickster wants. For example, some people offer to help elderly people invest their money and then abscond with their funds. Those who use the trickster pattern have terrifying and painful memories in their many black holes. They believe they will never be able to live the life they want. What they really want is love, but they do not believe love is possible, so they crave power instead.

A New York photographer met a young woman at a party through mutual friends. They enjoyed their conversation and he invited her to come to his studio. He offered to take a few pictures. He said he might be able to use them in some of his work. He indicated that he would enjoy her company and thought the pictures might help her get started in New York. She was flattered that he wanted pictures of her and was delighted to spend time with him. After he had taken a few photos, he invited her to take off her blouse. When she hesitated, he said, "You're a professional, aren't you?"

The photographer offered something the young woman wanted—attention and photographs—but there were strings attached. If his offer had been sincere, the young woman would have felt no pressure. As it was, she felt pressured into giving him what he asked for. This is the trickster pattern. In the beginning it's hard to tell the difference between the charmer and the trickster pattern, but the lack of genuine interest in the young woman implies a deeper need for power to mask the photographer's black holes.

A recent survey asked young men if they believed it was okay to tell a woman that they loved her in order to have sex with her. Nearly 80 percent said yes. This survey suggests that many young men are willing to play the charmer/trickster pirate pattern.

The person who uses this charmer/trickster pattern wants something. He may have sexual favors confused with power. He charms us. We soothe his fear that he can't get what he wants. He is driven to pirating to prove to himself that he can get what he wants, but no matter how much he gets, he never believes that he can truly have what he wants. He wants to feel empowered without our favors, but doesn't, so he continues to get what he can.

If the core fear in our own black hole is that we are not lovable, the charmer/trickster is hard to resist. He offers the love and attention we crave. Abusive men can be charming at first and attract women who have a desperate fear of being alone and unloved. His apologies and the promise of his attention are offered in exchange for the terror and physical abuse these women suffer.

Walking along the Oregon coastal highway near my coast house one day, I met a woman who had a black eye. Her face was red and bruised. Holding her little girl by the hand, she limped along. I asked her to tell me her story. For the past six years, she had been living with a man who beat her up regularly. She finally took her daughter and left him for what she thought was the final time. A few days later, he called her and accused her of taking the money they had hidden. She resolutely denied taking it. So he said, "Come show me where it is." She returned, found the money, and gave it to him. Then he beat her up again.

This man was not charming. He was playing the trickster. He set the bait by asking her to prove her truthfulness, then used her black hole to steal her power. Feeling unworthy she returned to prove her trustworthiness, then, he beat her up to feel powerful and anesthetize his black holes.

The charmer and trickster pirate patterns both offer something in exchange for what they want. The charmer has bottomless needs for acceptance, appreciation, and doing things his way. As long as he gets what he wants, he is charming. The trickster has a driving need to secure power over another person. He is not satisfied with anything less than the power to get what he wants. The trickster can deny the hurt he causes others because gaining power is the only thing that keeps his black holes quiet.

PERFORMER/COMEDIAN ENERGY PIRATE PATTERN

A person engaged in performer pirating thrives on the excitement of winning and the stimulation of recognition. She is terrified of failure. She is afraid she is loved only for her charm, image, success, and wit—for her performance. The performer is driven by her need to prove that she is capable, resourceful, and lovable—capable of succeeding, capable of winning, resourceful enough to create a life full of pleasure and excitement. What she really wants is to be loved and accepted for who she is even if she fails, but since she believes she's not enough and not lovable, she must not fail. Therefore, someone with the performer energy pirate pattern is driven to build a successful, exciting life. She will use her stage presence to create an image of a winner that we shower with attention. She works on her appearance to match her idealized self-image. She wins our attention, admiration, and appreciation by excelling at whatever she undertakes. A subcategory of the performer pirate pattern is the comedian pattern. The comedian is a true performer. She uses humor to entertain and pirate energy at the same time.

Here's an example. At work one day, Charlie felt the sting of performer pirating and later talked to his wife about it. "We had a meeting today to talk about the marketing program. I thought I'd be presenting the report since I did most of the work. I'm thinking it's going to be me handing out the report and talking about it, but my boss already had the report and said that Farah had been telling him about it! Then my boss started asking Farah questions. So, Farah explained *my* ideas, and I just sat there. I can't believe it. She really never has had any good ideas." His wife added, "But she recognized your good ideas."

"Farah makes me so mad. I just want to throttle her." His wife advised him, "There are a lot of people like Farah. You can't let her get to you."

"I just sat there feeling squashed," said Charlie. "When the meeting was over my boss walked out with Farah. I didn't know what to do."

Charlie had a black hole reaction when Farah took the credit for his work by stealing the acknowledgment he wanted. Charlie supported Farah in looking good by saying nothing. He will likely have another black hole reaction if Farah is promoted to the job that he wants.

We may enjoy performer pirating if the performance doesn't eclipse our own achievements. People with performer patterns can be outgoing, funny, goofy, outlandish, or knowledgeable. They may exaggerate to make themselves look good—claiming family money, college degrees, or high-powered positions they don't really have. We may be impressed, at first, by these claims. Impressing people energizes the person using performer pirating to get what he wants.

Some people playing performer pirate may deliberately do things to trouble others. They may tease, make a nuisance of themselves, make sexist comments, accentuate their bodily functions—burping, chewing, farting—boast of their escapades, and, in the extreme, master illegal activities in order to impress their peers.

Not everyone who calls attention to herself is engaged in performer pirating. Many celebrity performers give generously of themselves without craving the adulation. Other performers are addicted to the fanfare. Their need for energy urges them to be smarter, more important, more talented, more glamorous, more experienced, or more outrageous to gain the energy they need.

A subcategory of the performer energy pirate pattern is the comedian performer pattern. Someone playing the part of a comedian pirate creates energy by generating laughter using put-downs in the guise of fun. Laughter is a good feeling. The comedian and the audience both feel energized by the exchange, at the expense of the person or group that has been put down.

Like a challenge offered to duel, put-downs invite put-downs. If we respond with another put-down that is equally funny, we can reclaim our energy. It's a game—a pirate game.

One-liner challenges are a part of Western culture. The comedian pirate game is prevalent in organizations dominated by hierarchies. In the British Parliament, for example, put-downs are standard practice for determining who gets heard. It is a way to establish pecking order or dominance among co-workers and friends. I learned this game from my male colleagues in the electric power industry.

A mutual exchange of put-downs is sometimes used to strengthen friendships. One friend good-humoredly accepts being put down, handing over a little of his energy as a show of trust. The other friend then returns the favor. The comedian form of the performer pattern seems to be more prevalent among men. It's a way of saying, "You're okay." "I'm okay." For example, you may see two men greet each other, one will say, "Hey, party animal, what you been up to?" The other responds, "Not much, pretty boy." These jabs are not barbs. They have a function—to connect the two men. However, there is a very fine line between friendly barbs and pirating.

There are many other forms of humor. Not all comedians engage in pirating. Former U.S. Senator, Mo Udall, used humor to engage and connect. He used humor at his own expense, self-deprecating humor that encouraged others to laugh at him. Senator Udall also used humor to help us laugh together at ourselves. In contrast, the comedian pirate pattern employs humor to gain energy by putting others down. Gender, lawyer, and ethnic jokes are examples of humor that put down groups of people.

As a woman in a male-dominated industry, I felt challenged by put-downs and experienced a loss of energy each time someone captured the momentum with his humor at my expense. I developed a temporary coping strategy of returning the put-downs, as in the following exchanges.

"I didn't mean to disturb your nap." "Then it is okay to nap in these meetings."

"Did your mother dress you this morning?" "No, but I like what your wife picked out for you."

"When are you going to stay in my hotel room?" "I don't know how you keep hope alive, because things haven't changed that much."

"Did I interrupt you in the middle of my sentence?" "Some people just don't know they're through."

In each of these exchanges there's an attempt to even the energy score. Any response generally encourages the continuation of the pirating game. These games have the effect of keeping us on our toes, although not comfortably. There's always the possibility that we won't find a snappy comeback. The people who relish these games are typically the ones who are good at them. Someone may say, "That's one for me," or "one-up," and those who draw a one in the air are keeping an energy pirate score.

DISTANT/INDIFFERENT ENERGY PIRATE PATTERN

Someone using the distant/indifferent pirate pattern doesn't want to deal with other pirate control and manipulation strategies. So he pulls back and manipulates others into coming to him. He is afraid of being controlled by other people. He feels as though he doesn't fit in and thinks he may be crazy. By distancing himself, he can avoid being controlled and still draw attention from others.

Mike handled a crisis at work on Friday, played in a rough and tumble soccer game that evening, and arrived home exhausted. Saturday morning, he was sore and cranky. His wife, Pam, had hoped to get Mike's help fixing the kitchen faucet, and then go hiking together. It turned out to be a beautiful fall weekend. Pam realized that Mike needed time to relax and recover. She brushed aside his crankiness and gave Mike space to plant himself in front of the television. She tried to talk with him about his week and asked if he would help her with the leak. She also mentioned hiking. Mike said he would help later and then ignored her. She tried to get his attention by popping popcorn and bringing his dinner into the TV room. On Sunday afternoon, Mike was contented. Pam was exhausted.

On Monday morning, Mike was rejuvenated and ready to go back to work. Pam was tired and cranky, and wasn't ready to return to work. Mike didn't realize that he had sapped Pam's energy. Pam didn't realize that she had given her energy to Mike. Later, Pam came to see that she was afraid of rejection. When he was distant, she catered to him. Mike didn't want his moods to affect Pam, but he was happy to be taken care of in front of the television.

A person who is distancing himself may pretend he doesn't need anything or anyone. He may withdraw to observe and detach himself. He may require minimal worldly possessions so that he will not need anything from anyone. He may control us by his simply not being there for us, by being uncooperative or inaccessible. We may seek him out and feel frustrated that we can't get him to participate or contribute.

Family members will try to change, improve, and generally "fix" the person who wants distance. This means he gets attention energy from well-intended others. Usually, he will pretend that he doesn't want this kind of attention. And indeed, too much interest causes him to pull away even further.

A person playing the distant pirate pattern thinks that he knows more than other people do about life and at the same time is confused about what he really wants. He tells himself that he doesn't care what others think, but he feels lonely. He thinks he is above other people, but is afraid that he is different from everyone else. He gets what he wants by engaging others with the pretense of distance and indifference. He may even convince himself that he resents the attention, but if it goes away, he'll get it back.

James Redfield calls this type "aloof." He suggests that someone using the aloof control drama constantly creates a vague and mysterious aura around herself, forcing us to pour energy into digging to get information normally shared in a casual manner....It is a method of manipulation that seeks to lure us in, yet keep us at a distance.

Many teenagers go through a distancing phase. They are confused about who they are and use indifference to protect themselves from parents who haven't adjusted to having more independent children. When parents stop trying to control and improve their teenagers' behavior, usually the distancing goes away. Some people develop a black hole of fear from what seems like "madness" in their families. They use this energy strategy as a way to distance themselves from being manipulated.

Distancing/indifferent energy strategies cover up three basic fears: the fear of being too different, the fear of not being a loving person, and the fear of going insane. As long as someone is reaching out to him, he can protect his fears. Someone using this strategy takes energy from people reaching out and creates more distance. He reassures himself that if people reach out he must be okay.

ENERGY PIRATES ARE US

We may be tempted to point the finger at other people as energy pirates. As humans we have a tendency to label others. For example, if two people vociferously disagree, they might label each other intimidator energy pirates. I have provided these categories of energy pirating as a way to show some of the common patterns we find in human interaction. I am not suggesting that we label people. I hope you won't. Labeling separates and disconnects. Separation usually results in a loss of understanding and energy.

Rather than labeling others, I suggest that you ask yourself if any of these patterns fit you. I think we are each capable of all of the pirate patterns, but we probably have our favorites. Fortunately, we have more influence over our own behavior than that of other people. Pirate patterns are harder to recognize in ourselves, however, so it can be helpful to try to identify them in other people's behavior, and then look carefully at our own patterns. It was easier for me to find these pirate patterns in my children, my dad, my boss, and my spouse than in myself. I didn't really want to look at my own pirate patterns because doing so could trigger a black hole. Once a black hole is triggered, we have a fundamental choice. We can choose to recognize and explore the black hole, or we can mask it by running pirate patterns and stealing enough energy from others to escape its grip. Both choices have consequences.

Exploring our black holes is the way to release them and align our creative energy, but this route is less familiar to most people. We are more likely to choose an unconscious pirate pattern—the familiar route. With this choice, we can expect the reactions that we typically get from others. We are usually not even aware of making this choice because the familiarity of the patterns makes them seem normal. It's like growing up without enough to eat; you may believe that feeling hungry is normal. Most of us choose to pirate energy from others rather than explore our black holes. At the same time, we would prefer that others release their black holes rather than pirate our energy.

In general, every one of us is doing the best we can with the black holes we have. Most of us are not aware of how our hidden assumptions, expectations, beliefs, and emotions call forth the reactions we get from others in our energy field. Our black holes invite energy pirating. People stuck in pirate patterns react quite differently with someone who doesn't have as many fears and false beliefs hidden away.

We have black holes and are surrounded by people with black holes. In order to protect ourselves, we may blame others, counterattack, defend our reactions, or distract ourselves from noticing our black holes. Unfortunately, none of these defenses protect us from energy loss. They just shift our awareness away from our black holes. Most of us don't want an energy pirate triggering our black holes, so we defend ourselves because we don't know what else to do.

As human beings we are always vulnerable. We have a full range of vulnerable emotions that emerge when we feel threatened. We experience feeling vulnerable when we share our deep feelings and misgivings. Vulnerability by itself is not a terrifying experience to be avoided, though it can feel that way. Vulnerability is a rare and beautiful quality that connects us with others. Think of how we are drawn to babies. Their energy is vulnerable and open, no defenses, no addictions, no lies, only the truth of their being: hungry, distressed, happy, contented. How they feel and what they want is not hidden.

When we feel vulnerable, however, energy pirating strategies expand and deepen our sense of vulnerability. Children unprotected by caution, suspicion, and skepticism are vulnerable to pirating strategies. We learned to protect our vulnerabilities from the pirating we experienced in our early lives.

Vulnerabilities cry out to be held gently with reassurance and understanding. When instead, we encounter pirating, we bury our tender emotions and desires. We hide our vulnerabilities in our black holes. Though our intention is protection, when we hide tender feelings and desires, we diminish our creativity and our connection with each other.

What we didn't know as children was how to hold our vulnerable experiences in the context of our whole lives. Our observer self, the small voice inside us that speaks to us in quiet moments, can acknowledge our vulnerabilities and our strengths at the same time. Instead of protecting ourselves with pirating patterns, we are protected by the energy of our whole beings. Our observer knows that we are vulnerable and also strong, that we can feel both scared and brave, that we can feel threatened and be resourceful. By developing our observer selves we can share our vulnerabilities with a sense of strength and resourcefulness.

We take up energy pirating to defend ourselves and to gain the energy that comes with getting what we want. What we want is influenced by what energy state we are in. In a more balanced and aligned energy state, our personal desires are few. We may want to serve or contribute. This state of joy is our natural energy state. Free of the influence of black holes, we feel lovable, capable, resourceful, and empowered. We are both loved and loving. Life has an easy flow.

The usual energy state of most of us, however, is a blend of this natural, balanced, loving energy state and our black holes. Keeping our emotional memories hidden kinks our energy. In our usual energy state, we want many things: more money, more time off, a better job, different friends. We want others to make our lives more comfortable. In this energy state, we are subject to energy pirating.

People who believe that they have no black holes are more strongly influenced by their emotional stories and beliefs than people who acknowledge their black holes and realize when one is influencing them. People who have released and accepted their black holes have more balanced energy. They are less likely to react to energy pirating because their black holes are rarely triggered. If people pirating energy can't trigger their black holes, the pirating doesn't work. People who have balanced and aligned their creative energy are safe from energy pirating.

Chapter Four

How Can You Discover a Black Hole?

· ·

Kathy was the supervisor of new accounts for a bank. When her boss, Ed, talked to her about improving her department, Kathy resisted his ideas and resented his intrusion. She thought he was domineering and didn't take time to understand him. She felt singled out and alone. On his part, Ed was uncomfortable with Kathy, even though he valued her work. Although she worked hard, her attitude toward him strained their relationship. When Ed was promoted to branch manager, Kathy applied for his old job. She had been in the branch longer than anyone else and was knowledgeable about banking. Several other people in the branch also applied. All of them were interviewed by the selection team, of which Ed was a part. Skip, who had been in the branch only a few months, was chosen to be Kathy's new boss. Kathy called her husband and told him she thought she might resign. Her husband suggested that she talk with me.

She felt rejected and inadequate and, as we talked, she remembered feeling controlled by her mother when she was growing up. She explored her feelings as a young girl and the decisions she had made about herself. In order to get what she wanted, she believed she had to resist people's attempts to control her. She re-experienced how powerless she felt and how angry she was. Her stomach felt tense and a little nauseous as she explored that black hole. She sensed that the intensity of her reaction to Ed was the same as her reaction to her mother. She recognized that her resentment and resistance had affected her relationship with Ed. She took responsibility for her judgments and her actions, which helped her see how she had influenced Ed's decision.

Black hole reactions are disguised as normal life patterns, and that's why we don't notice them. Their purpose is to hide what we don't want to experience. The black holes have such ordinary triggers that we are often unaware of them until a serious accident, an illness, or the loss of an important relationship calls our attention to the hidden fear and pain in our lives.

I think most of us have emotional stories tucked away. We naturally want to protect our vulnerabilities. When we find and release our black holes, we no longer need to protect ourselves through energy pirating or pretending we are something we're not. If you think you may have hidden emotional stories and would like to find your black holes, there are guides to help you.

Think about how you would like to handle a black hole before you find one, so that you will feel safe if one of your black holes is triggered. Your plan may be as simple as writing down your experience and meditating. You may ask friends for support (see the next chapter). Once you have decided how you can feel safe, you can go on and look for your black holes. The job is easier when you know what you're looking for. There are four indicators that will help you recognize a black hole: emotional intensity, critical judgments, physical symptoms, and spiritual disconnection.

In the story above, Kathy resented Ed's suggestions (emotional intensity). She was critical of Ed and judged him as "domineering" (critical judgment). Her stomach hurt as she struggled with Ed's suggestions (physical symptoms), and she felt alone in her resistance (spiritual disconnection). Some black holes have only one or two indicators; some have three or four. Kathy's had all four indicators.

EMOTIONAL INTENSITY AS AN INDICATOR OF A BLACK HOLE

You'll know that you have found a black hole when you react to a situation more intensely than is logically called for. Here are some common examples that may indicate the presence of a black hole: getting angry or upset over small things; feeling panicky in social situations; feeling hurt when your friends get together without you; feeling terrible when you make a mistake. If you feel depressed, you may have several black holes. The key to finding your black holes is to notice your own reaction. If your reaction is a spike off the baseline of your normal experience, you can follow your reaction to a black hole.

Think of your normal emotional state when you are talking with your friends, working, shopping for food—your usual routine. Consider the experience of these activities your normal emotional baseline. Something that puts a bulge in that baseline indicates a black hole. Intense emotional feelings include hostility, grief, terror, rage, humiliation, shame, and guilt, among others. Guilt is feeling bad about something you've done or haven't done, while shame is feeling bad about who you are.

Feeling intensely excited about a date could indicate a black hole. Feeling hopeless, helpless, or worthless also suggests a black hole. The key is the intensity of your reaction, compared to the reality of the trigger. If I ask you how you are, and you burst into tears, your reaction is out of proportion to the trigger—my inquiry after your health. If you make some suggestions about how I might improve my skiing and I wonder if I will ever learn to ski, my reaction is more intense than the suggestions warrant. These intense emotional reactions probably indicate a black hole. A black hole is apparent when something inside of us is agitated and ready to pop, like a pressure cooker ready to blow its top. My mother once had an overheated pressure cooker cover the kitchen ceiling with mashed potatoes when it blew out its contents. It was a mirror for how she was feeling that day.

Track your own emotional baseline and notice your reactions. An emotional spike or bulge can help you find your black holes. Here is a story illustrating an emotionally intense reaction that indicates a black hole.

———— · · · · · ————

In a workshop Dave had just released a black hole with Debra's help. She told him what she had learned from helping him. I asked him if he would like a little space to integrate his experience. He was grateful for my suggestion.

When Debra grew quiet, I asked her what had happened. "You just triggered a black hole. When you asked if Dave wanted space, my reaction was huge. I felt as though I'd been slapped in the face and told to shut up! My reaction was way out of proportion to what you said, so it must be a black hole."

I asked her if she remembered a time in her childhood when she felt that way. She answered, "I'm scared that I can't do it right. After all my years of training, I still don't know when to shut up. I just babble on and on, not knowing when to stop. I felt this way before with my dad. I could never satisfy him. He found something wrong with everything I did."

I asked her whether there was a picture or scene where she could see him talking to her. "Not really. The only scene I can see is on the beach and he's not talking to me. He's just pushing me away."

Dave asked her how old she was and what was happening. "I was an energetic, talkative four-year-old. My dad's reading the paper. I'm singing and trying to get him to play with me. He pushes me away and says, 'Be quiet. You talk too much.'"

I asked her how she felt at that moment. "I'm stunned. He was never like that before. I must have done something wrong. I talk too much. I'm a pest."

I asked her whether she felt the same way today about me when I asked Dave if he wanted to be quiet. "I was talking too much. I should have noticed when Dave needed space."

Dave asked how that experience on the beach was different from the experience today with the three of us. "My dad's gone, but I'm still hurting."

I asked where she hurt. "My chest hurts," Debra replied, putting a hand over her heart. We encouraged Debra to breathe into her heart, and sat with her while she did. Dave and I asked a few more questions to help her explore her black hole. We accepted her experience and stayed with her until she was feeling better.

Without recognizing the emotional intensity of her reaction, Debra might not have found her black hole. Her intense reaction led to her hidden pain. By exploring her black hole, she was able to release it .

CRITICAL JUDGMENT AS AN INDICATOR OF A BLACK HOLE

Critical judgment is a mental process. When you recognize your own critical judgment, it's a way of identifying a black hole. This process prompts a powerful shift in understanding. It's easy to think that we are right while viewing others as wrong. Critical thoughts include blaming others; judging, labeling, discounting them; and wanting them to change. They basically are defensive strategies. Judgment and blaming keep us from feeling our tender emotions and diverts attention from our black holes. For example, you may have concluded that someone at work is the reason why you aren't more successful or that your spouse is stopping you from doing what you'd really like to do. This stance keeps you from seeing how your own black holes are holding you back.

When we focus our attention on others, we're not so focused on our own shortcomings. We can protect ourselves from seeing the part we play in the situations in our life. If we acknowledge that we made a mistake or said something unkind, we fear we may trigger one of our black holes. By blaming others, discounting them, and thinking that they should change, we avoid our own triggers.

Normally, people who judge others don't realize how their judgments protect them from finding their black holes. When I shifted from judging and blaming others to seeing my own pain and confusion it was hard at first. When I began to experience my black holes, I felt scared and vulnerable. Judgment was easier. Encouraging people to look at their judgments to find hidden emotional memories is like suggesting that accountants play in a rock band. Some are able to do it, others aren't. Many people don't see the value in experiencing their own vulnerabilities. They are too afraid of their own emotional reactions to consider the possibility that their judgments really aren't about other people, but about themselves.

Critical judgment serves as a mirror. If there is someone you would like to change, that person can help you find your black holes.

People with balanced energy generally accept others as they are. If we are at peace with ourselves, we have compassion for others. The more we accept ourselves, the more we accept others. Our critical judgments are valuable guides for finding what we don't accept about ourselves. Even seemingly inconsequential judgments can point to a black hole.

———————— • • • • • ————————

This story of critical judgment and its effects involves Debra and Dave again, along with Phil, from the same workshop as in the previous story. Dave was frustrated with the meetings at work because they never started on time. He was punctual, in itself an admirable trait. Dave judged others who weren't on time. "It's rude to be late. It's such a waste of people's time, but it seems to bother me more than other people. When we don't start on time, I feel tense and anxious, it takes a while for me to warm up before I can help people solve their problems."

Phil and Debra agreed to help trigger Dave's black hole by inventing a scene. Dave left the room, so Phil and Debra could plan the trigger. When Dave came back, Debra was gone. Phil began the conversation. "We can't start the meeting until Debra gets back. I realize that you have to meet with the vice president in five minutes, but Debra is bringing crucial information the vice president needs. I'm sure she'll be right back." Phil talked to me then about the weather and his vacation plans. When Dave started looking at his watch and getting restless, Debra finally returned. "Have you guys been waiting for me? You won't believe what I just heard in the hallway," and she shared the latest company gossip. Phil pretended to be absorbed in the gossip, but after a few minutes, Dave's black hole was triggered. "I'm there and I'm feeling tense and anxious. I want you two to shut up. Give me the information I need and let me get to my meeting with the VP. I can't believe you are going on about that old gossip when I've got something important to do. Boy, am I judging you!"

I asked if he could think of a time he felt this way before, perhaps when he was a kid. "No, not really, only when people at work are late for a meeting. I do this a lot."

Phil asked where Dave grew up. "In Utah, in the desert."

Phil then asked what Dave liked to do there. "I loved hiking out in the desert. I'd be out there all day if they'd let me."

Debra asked if he ever felt this way out in the desert? "No, I loved it out there, but when my dad called, I'd better be within earshot or I'd get whipped."

I asked how he liked having to say close to hear his dad call. "I hated it, but I knew better than to be late."

Phil asked how this current situation was like when Dave was a kid. Tears moistened Dave's eyes. He rested his forehead in his hand. Debra asked what was happening. "My dad whipped Ray, my oldest brother, until he was bleeding, but my dad didn't stop. Ray was screaming. There was blood. I was so scared. I just stood there. Dad looked over at me and said, 'Now I don't want you boys ever to be late. You hear me?' I was so scared. I wanted to run to Ray, but my dad said, 'No, leave him be.'" We sat together quietly, open to hearing and not judging Dave's experience.

Phil asked Dave if his dad ever hit him. "No, he didn't have to. I never went out in the desert where I really wanted to go. I limited my exploration to remaining within earshot and I was always there when he called. I gave up my freedom. I gave up what I really wanted because of my dad."

I asked how that situation was different from the one today. "Well, my dad died a few years ago, but I still limit my freedom just like I did then. I wanted a nice car, but we got a practical station wagon for the family. I wanted to go to the desert for our vacation, but we went to Disneyland for the kids. I don't really let myself have what I want."

Phil asked whether he still felt anxious about time. "Yeah, I still want to be on time. But I guess I don't want to feel so tense about it, and if someone else is late...well, I don't know."

"You know, Dave, I'm almost always late for meetings," Debra admitted. "I don't do it out of disrespect for your time or anyone else's. I just get so caught up in trying to get one more thing done. I'm trying to satisfy a lot of people and I can't ever please all of them. I know being on time is important to you and I don't want to trouble you, but sometimes I just don't get it together. I'd like a little slack when I'm under so much pressure." Dave responded, "I think I understand. I'd like to give myself a little grace once in a while too."

I asked how he was feeling right now. "I'm feeling looser, a little freer. I'm surprised that such a small thing could have so much connected to it. I'm thinking I might even talk to my wife about a new car."

Dave used his judgment about people who aren't on time to find and explore a black hole. Now he has more awareness of his pattern and can see more choices. He still wants to be on time and wants others to honor their time commitments, but he no longer feels so rigid about slip-ups. More importantly, he realized that he had been limiting his own freedom.

——————— • • • • • ———————

We judge others for what we don't like in ourselves. For example, when people at work speak in anger, we may be critical of them for not controlling their temper, even though at home we sometimes speak in anger. People who need to be in control are often critical of the boss or others who are controlling. We may judge someone who brags because we don't respect ourselves when we brag about our accomplishments.

We may pacify our critical judgment about ourselves by feeling guilty. In feeling guilty, we punish ourselves a little for something we have done. Guilt helps us assuage our disappointment about what we did. We may not be so generous with others. For example, if we give away our power by doing things we don't really want to do so that someone will like us, we may be critical of others who do the same thing. We may not want to associate with them because they do what we don't like about ourselves.

When we recognize a critical judgment, it's an opportunity to ask ourselves, "How am I like that? Do I have any tendencies to be like that, even a little? Do I feel bad about myself when I do that?"

It's an opportunity to explore the origin of our limitations. Even though we may continue to act in the same way, we will have more understanding and awareness of our choices. This awareness will give us more compassion for others and ourselves.

We judge others for what we don't allow ourselves to do. We may have been influenced by our parents to be on time, as Dave was. We may judge others for being late because we are afraid of that tendency in ourselves. We don't give other people or ourselves any slack when it comes to our internally imposed rules. If we are afraid that we might be like them, but are afraid to explore within ourselves to find the truth, we may turn our fear into anger and judgment.

For example, at one time I was judgmental about and afraid of gay people. Then I learned that a longtime dear friend of mine was a lesbian. I was shaken by her revelation, and it caused me to do some soul searching. Part of that search was to consider my own preferences. I was afraid to even think about it at first, afraid of what I might find. But remaining unaware was pushing me toward rejecting my friend. I considered the possibility in my mind that I myself might be attracted to women. By allowing my fear, I realized that though I love my women friends, I am clearly attracted to men. Secure in my sexual orientation, I was able to accept my friend's choice and continue to enjoy her friendship. If I hadn't explored my own preference, I might have covered up my fear by judging and rejecting my friend. I would have continued to be afraid of gay people and might have unconsciously rejected other people who are different from me. In the extreme, this fear is covered by hatred.

We judge those who are doing what we would like to do. We may judge others because we wish we were like them. We might like to be rich or famous. We might like to have the power that politicians have. We might like to have the professional respect accorded doctors and lawyers. If we don't have money, power, respect, recognition, or prestige, we may judge others who do. We may tell ourselves that rich people aren't happy. We may believe that their lives are driven by greed so that they never spend time with their families. We may tell jokes that put down doctors, lawyers, and politicians. By judging, we feel better about not having achieved what they have. By judging, we can remain unaware that we are envious. By judging, we can ignore the part of us that would like to be rich and powerful, and avoid facing the part of us that feels like a failure because we are not. Our fear of failure is a black hole. Recognizing our judgment can lead us to our black holes and ultimately to acceptance of ourselves and those we have judged.

We judge those we don't understand. The difference between you and people of other cultures, religions, or ethnic backgrounds can seem threatening because you don't understand them. Most of us have black holes anchored in religion, school, and community. Exploring these black holes gives you a new view of the context of your life. You may have made choices about where you live and the work you do based on the expectations and limitations of your background. Exploring these black holes offers you a greater understanding of your life choices. With greater understanding, you can then choose either not to change something or consider other options.

When we are at peace with our cultural heritage and our spiritual path, we need not feel threatened by different practices and beliefs. These differences add richness and texture to life. By releasing our black holes, we can become curious observers and diligent students of others' life choices, willing to learn new steps for our own spiritual journey. If you find yourself critical of people, look first to see if you sometimes do what they do, wish you could do, are afraid of doing, or don't understand what you see in them.

Another way to find your own emotional intensity or critical judgment is to look for an abrupt shift in your experience. You may find yourself blaming others, and then proceed to blame yourself. These are polar shifts. I have noticed my own thinking shift from "it's all your fault" to "it's all my fault" and back again in a matter of minutes. I call switching from one extreme to the other the polar pirate effect. Not everyone experiences it, but I bring it to your attention because if you notice this effect, you can be sure there's a black hole. Here are some other examples of the polar pirate effect:

- Feeling great about yourself followed by feeling terrible about yourself
- Making demands of others, then later feeling guilty about being demanding
- Showering someone with love and attention, then discounting him
- Offering to give someone a gift, then wishing you hadn't
- Physically abusing your spouse, later feeling sorry and ashamed

If you suffer from the polar pirate effect, notice what happens when you stop dancing your pirate dance from pole to pole. Hold both extremes in your conscious attention at once. This isn't easy. It may jangle your thinking. Your body may shake a little. Holding both will allow your feelings to merge. Then your sensations and emotions will lead you to a black hole. You can release your polar pirate black hole by following one of the release processes described in the next chapter.

PHYSICAL SYMPTOMS AS AN INDICATOR OF A BLACK HOLE

Black holes manifest physically due to the mind-body link. Our mind, emotions, desires, and physical bodies are all one energetic system. Our emotional memories are physically located in our energy fields. Muscles, tissues, and internal organs are often the physical location of black holes. Symptoms that accompany a black hole experience include physical discomfort, headaches, dizziness, tension, aches, pains, emptiness, pressure, weight problems, sudden exhaustion, sleeping problems, and feeling unusually warm or cold. All of these can also indicate medical problems, and sometimes it is hard to tell the difference. If you have been to a doctor and haven't found the source of your symptoms, consider the possibility that a black hole is disturbing your energy field and causing those symptoms.

If you have headaches regularly or a nervous stomach and

digestive system, your tension might be from a black hole. If you have heart or lower back problems, you might want to consider black hole involvement. These areas are commonly affected by black holes in your energy system. If it is a black hole, your symptoms will increase when it is triggered; and when you release the black hole, the symptoms will diminish or disappear.

While some of these physical symptoms, such as shoulder tension or not sleeping well, are chronic, most symptoms connected to black holes come and go. They may be stronger at one time of the day, as is often the case with headaches. They may appear monthly (menstrual cramps) or come and go with the seasons (holiday anxiety or arthritis pain). Some may be associated with locations such as your family home or the dentist office. Perhaps heights or small places tend to produce a flare-up of your symptoms. All of these associations are clues to the hidden emotional stories in your black holes.

Black holes that produce physical symptoms are easier to find. When you experience physical discomfort, ask yourself what message it has for you. Your mind will attempt to answer any question. Observe your thoughts and emotions. If you feel anger, sadness, or fear, you have probably found a black hole. Allowing yourself to feel your emotions will help you release blocked emotional stories. Meditation and breathing can alone release black holes. Anger, sadness, and fear are normal, healthy emotions. Experiencing them will help you keep from hiding your emotions in a black hole. After you have released a black hole, notice whether your symptoms have changed. If you feel better—more comfortable, lighter, freer, stronger—this indicates that release has occurred. The next story describes some of the physical symptoms that indicate a black hole.

——————— · · · · · ———————

Maggie believed that she held her stress in her shoulders causing her neck to be stiff and sore much of the time. Her friend Tanya encouraged her to explore the physical discomfort. Maggie drew inward, focusing on the pressure in her neck and shoulders. She sat quietly, allowing the discomfort by not resisting it, or trying to ignore it, or trying to make it go away. As she focused on the tension in her shoulders, Maggie's cheeks flushed and her neck broke out in splotchy red patches.

Tanya asked when Maggie felt this way before. "I remember something when I was very young. I don't remember what happened. I just remember my mom yelling, 'Stop crying.' She's mad. I feel small and scared. My mom says, 'Don't ever do that again. No more crying.'"

Tanya asked whether Maggie could see herself. "Yes, I'm standing there in my pink striped shirt and my pink shorts. My shoulders are hunched up. I'm trying to keep from crying." Maggie's forehead wrinkled, she squeezed her eyelids shut, but couldn't keep her tears from seeping out. Leaning forward, with her hands over her face, she wept. Tanya sat quietly with her.

When Maggie started breathing more easily, she said, "I haven't cried since I was three years old. I never saw my mother or her mother cry. I feel ashamed, like I've broken a vow."

Tanya asked how her shoulders and neck were. "They still hurt, but not as much."

Maggie and Tanya continued talking. Tanya listened and openly considered everything Maggie said. A half-hour later, Maggie was feeling less pressure. She had given herself permission to cry. The tension in her neck and shoulders was still there, but it had eased. Later, Maggie discovered other memories attached to the tension and discomfort in her neck and shoulders.

The physical discomfort that Maggie had discounted as normal became a doorway to discovering hidden memories and emotions trapped in her black holes. Exploring her memories and accepting her emotions allowed Maggie to let go of some of her physical tension. Not all physical discomfort is this easy to unravel, but physical symptoms can help us connect with painful emotional stories and release our black holes.

———— · · · · · ————

Spiritual Disconnection As an Indicator of a Black Hole

If you feel alone in trying to create the life you want, you may be disconnected from the universal flow of spiritual energy. Black holes can diminish our spiritual energy by hiding our spiritual beliefs. Our connection to balanced spiritual energy can be severely limited. We may have put away our spiritual beliefs because they didn't make logical sense, or because we were made to participate in religious practices we didn't believe in. Our spiritual connection can be blocked by emotional memories. If you feel disconnected from spiritual energy, follow your fears about God and spirituality to discover how you are limiting your spiritual energy.

——————— • • • • • ———————

Stacey was struggling with her new business, cranial-sacral massage. She wasn't earning enough money to live on. When she came to talk with me, she was feeling scared and alone. She was pursuing her new work without help or support from friends, and no one in her family understood what she was trying to do. In her heart she believed in her mission to help people, but she was scared she wouldn't be able to breathe life into her dream. She was tempted to go back to work in the real estate office that had drained her energy. They wanted her back, but she had spent several years training for cranial-sacral massage and didn't want to give up her dream.

I asked her to let herself feel the vulnerability and isolation she had been experiencing. Then I asked where in her body she felt scared that her business wouldn't survive. "It seems to be on the left side of my body." Stacey put her hand on the left side of her face. "This side of my face, my left shoulder and my arm, and all the way down my left leg."

I asked her what it felt like. "Just kind of dead, like it's not really animated. I don't know. It's hard to describe."

I asked her to close her eyes and breathe into the left side of her body. Stacey's tears came easily. I sat quietly with her. "I feel lost and alone. I'm in a very dark place," she said after a couple of minutes.

I asked her to keep her eyes closed and to notice if there was anything she could see in her mind's eye. "The darkness is getting lighter. It's kind of dark gray now." After a while she said, "There's a very thin shaft of light coming in over there."

I encouraged her to go over and see what it was. Stacey grabbed the Kleenex box and held several tissues to her face as she wept. After a few minutes, I asked her what it was. "It's my connection to God. It's always been there, I just didn't see it before. I am connected. We're all connected to God. All I have to do is be willing to find it."

I asked how she was feeling right now. "I'm feeling really sad, but more hopeful, sad that I didn't know I was connected. But I think I really did know—I was just afraid and doubted whether there really was a God. I wanted it to be true, and now I know there is a spiritual connection for me. How do I keep this feeling so that I don't go back to doubting again?"

I asked her about her old connection with God. "I was afraid there was no God."

I then asked her what she would like to believe. "I would like to believe that God is always with me," she responded.

I continued, "Let's make up a belief pair and expand your thinking so that when you're scared you can remember that both are true." She asked how we would do that. I asked her to repeat this phrase: "Even though I'm afraid there is no God, God is always with me." "Even though I'm afraid there is no God, God is always with me," Stacey repeated. "I like that."

I said, "Follow my hand with your eyes while you repeat that phrase for about a minute. That will distract your thinking and let your mind expand to hold both beliefs." I moved my hand back and forth in a sideways figure eight or infinity sign pattern in front of Stacey. Eye movement is known to assist in emotional release. After Stacey repeated the belief pair for a minute, following my hand movements with her eyes, I asked how she felt. "I'm feeling really peaceful. My left side feels tingly and more alive. I don't want to live my life without God's presence. I hope I can find it again when I want to," she said.

Several months later, after some work on other black holes, Stacey had all the clients she wanted and was easily supporting herself. Her black hole had blocked her spiritual connection. She called this energy God. I believe there are many names for our spiritual source of energy. Allowing spiritual energy to support us can help us feel less isolated and more connected to our dreams. Noticing a spiritual disconnection can be helpful in finding a black hole that is blocking your energy. As you release your black holes, renewed spiritual energy pours into your energy field. The light, good feeling you have after releasing a black hole is aligned spiritual energy. (See Chapter 8 for more about aligning with the flow of spiritual energy.)

——— · · · · · ———

FINDING A BLACK HOLE THROUGH A CRISIS

Black holes contribute to creating personal crises in our lives. For example, in the first story in this chapter, Kathy's reaction to her boss reduced her chances of success. She tried to deny her black hole by resenting and judging Ed. As a result of her behavior, she didn't get the position she wanted. Many times our own behavior, driven by our black holes, influences how others respond to us. The information in our energy fields attracts experiences that match the secret beliefs in our black holes. We may be unaware of the part we play, but we are full participants.

Personal tragedy is an opportunity to notice our emotional intensity, critical judgments, physical symptoms, and spiritual disconnections more easily. When we encounter serious personal difficulties, our bodies protect us at first by going into shock. Physical shock switches off our emotional reactions, keeping us from feeling overwhelmed. We may feel numb for a few hours, a few weeks, or perhaps months. Our responses go on automatic as we handle immediate needs.

When the shock begins to wear off, our physical, mental, and emotional reactions emerge. This is when we are tempted to create new black holes to stuff the intensity of our reactions away. We can protect our vulnerable feelings with resentment and blame, but this creates more to deal with and recover from. If, instead, we allow our intense reactions, we can find old black holes that relate to our current tragedy. It's normal to want to blast others for their part in the tragedy that has befallen us, but how we respond is a choice. We can try to cover our pain with resentment and blame, or we can use our reactions to find hidden emotional memories. We can talk honestly about what happened and how others have contributed. Being human, we are likely to feel some resentment and blame. Accepting these feelings and talking honestly about them with others will help us find our hidden emotional memories.

Acceptance of what happened and how we felt physically and emotionally is what allows us to release a tragedy without creating a black hole. In order to accept what happened we must also take responsibility for any blame or judgment we have about ourselves or others involved in what happened. Other black holes may be triggered as we recognize and allow our reactions. Talking about what happened with others who are involved can help us determine our part in the tragedy and help others take responsibility for how they contributed. Speaking honestly about our emotions can feel scary and difficult, but if we do, those emotions change and move beyond what happened.

Personal crises can be a catalyst for transformation, healing, and acceptance. Albert Einstein once said, "The significant problems we face can never be resolved at the level of thinking that created them." Talking, feeling, and thinking about our experiences differently allow access to hidden information that may be part of the solution to our difficulties. Acknowledging our experiences in a new way opens options that we couldn't see before.

Choosing to explore our reactions rather than blaming others can be personally wrenching and difficult. One of my most painful experiences was when I was fired from the utility company, the story at the beginning of this book. I tell more of my story here to share my personal experience in learning how difficult it is to turn critical judgment and emotional intensity into a search for black holes. I hope that something in my story will encourage you to join me on this incredibly painful, but rewarding journey to spiritual freedom.

I sat in my living room by myself, surrounded by flowers and cards of condolence sent by friends and supporters. The phone wasn't ringing as often as it had at first. I had been home for three days. At 2:30 that afternoon, one of the managers at the utility called. Mat was an engineer, not given to sharing personal thoughts or feelings. His voice was gentle as he asked how I was doing. "The people in energy conservation asked me to call and tell you that we miss you. I think we took for granted how much you supported us, and we didn't stop to appreciate the price you were paying for giving us support. Mostly I called to tell you thanks. Thanks for the opportunity to be doing what I'm doing now. Thanks for everything I learned from you. I'll miss you."

My throat knotted. I mumbled my appreciation and hung up the phone. I felt the fabric of my life unraveling. My head pounded, and my mind swirled like a strobe. I steadied myself on the kitchen counter, longing for the people I had depended on to manage the utility. I ached to be with my team. I could see myself walking across the mauve carpet, my secretary grinning at me from her desk. I pictured myself on the balcony overlooking the river where I had thought through the issues that eventually threw me from office. I realized for the first time that I was not going back to the job I loved, the job that was the fulfillment of my life's dream.

Trembling, I stumbled upstairs to my room and crumpled on the bed. I couldn't catch my breath and my body felt as though I had been hit by a car. I felt lost, alone, cut off from the people whose dreams I shared, the team I had gone to the mat for, the people I loved. I struggled for breath that came in choked sobs. I felt as though I had lost all my friends in battle. The cold reality of my dreams dying, my work relationships dying, and my power dying made me feel as if my life as I knew it was dying. Curled in a fetal position, grieving, shivering, aching, I soaked my pillow through with tears until I lay still and lifeless staring at the ceiling in my darkening bedroom.

I plunged into a black hole that afternoon. At the time, I didn't know what black holes were. I hated feeling vulnerable and hopeless, but I was pitched into the exact feelings I was avoiding.

Lost in grief, I faced the fact that I didn't believe in myself. I had worked my way to the top post of the utility to prove that I was capable. Fear that I was inadequate had fueled my rise. When I explored my black hole, I found in my own family a bias against women, a bias I rebelled against. "I'm as good as my brothers and I'll prove it," I reassured myself while I was growing up, not really believing it. I set out with my ego in the lead, but no matter how much I achieved, I couldn't prove to myself that I was enough. I didn't realize I had to believe in myself first, and when I did believe in myself there was no need to prove myself. But that understanding came much later.

Within four months the three commissioners who fired me were replaced with new board members, and I was given an opportunity to reapply for my old job. It was a tough decision. I felt drawn to return. I had loved my job and the people I worked with, but my desire for time to explore and learn about myself was stronger. Over the next few years I learned that each of us is lovable and capable just the way we are. I believe that we each have the right combination of abilities to fulfill our purpose in life. And when our souls are strong enough, we will know this is true, and then we simply are, and proving matters no more.

At times, I still feel scared or think I need to prove myself. I still have that within me. It's been a big part of my life, but it takes over less often now. I have a favorite phrase for when I catch myself feeling that way, "Oh well, I do that sometimes." Now, I have other choices beyond my black holes.

Each of us encounters personal trauma, it's part of life. Within the fear, grief, and loss is a vulnerable spot to be discovered that will strengthen our souls and lead each of us to a profound understanding of our purpose here. This silver lining can be lost if we distract ourselves with pointing fingers and placing blame. It can be lost if we melt down into our shame and fear. Personal tragedy is devastating enough without missing the gift it brings.

Visiting our black holes reveals important emotional memories and decisions—moments when we decided it wasn't safe to be all of who we are. We chose to limit ourselves in some way—to shut off some of our options because we felt hurt or someone close to us was harmed. These limiting decisions and beliefs led us to adopt automatic patterns. Exploring the situations that created the limiting decisions allows us to change the patterns. This process can be painful and terrifying, but once we've faced our pain and fear, black holes no longer control us. We can choose to keep our limiting beliefs and decisions, or we can choose to change them.

The children we were and all the experiences of our childhood are still with us. Our unconscious memories hold elaborate details of our personal history. Everything we have ever experienced—done, seen, heard, tasted, smelled, or felt—is still a part of us. Even when we release black holes, our emotions and memories are still part of us, but they no longer unconsciously rule our lives. When a black hole is triggered, although it tugs at us to react automatically, the way we have in the past, we do have other choices.

I invite you to join me in noticing your emotional intensity, critical judgment, physical symptoms, and spiritual disconnection to find and release your black holes. Knowing how to find hidden emotional memories can give us the freedom to go beyond the compulsive denial of our black holes. We can face our black holes and claim them, or keep them hidden and react automatically. The choice is ours.

Chapter Five

Exploring and Releasing Black Holes

·····················

Gena had been the news anchor for one of the most popular news stations in Portland, Oregon. She lost her job after taking an extended medical leave for cancer surgery. Gena blamed Rick, the station manager, for not keeping her high-profile job open while she recovered. She had tried hard to please him, and she expected him to take care of her.

───── · · · · · ─────

I met Gena three months after she lost her job when she came to one of my workshops. I asked her and two other persons at the workshop, Casey and Vince, to think of someone they were having difficulty with. I expected Gena to name Rick, her former manager. She slipped her hand over her mouth. Vince asked her whom she was thinking of. She shook her head. Her eyes filled with tears, and she whispered, "The person I have the most difficulty with is me. I'm my biggest problem."

Vince asked if she would be willing to talk with herself. "I don't know how." Gena's eyes darted around the room. "I want to work on this, but I don't know what to do." Casey asked if she wanted to be helped by us. She nodded.

I asked Gena who in the group was most like her, who could play her part. She looked at the three of us. Gena hesitated and then asked me to do it. I responded, "I'd be happy to be you. Tell me what you see in me that is like you—all the things you don't like about yourself." "I don't know. I see so much that I don't like." Gena grimaced.

With encouragement from Vince and Casey, she continued. "You're nice to people so they will approve of you. You got to where you are by being good-looking and playing up to people. You never got your degree, you didn't stick to it—maybe you're not smart enough to get a degree." I answered, playing my part, "I didn't have to get a degree, because people gave me what I wanted."

"That's right, and there's another thing. You crave approval. You're a suck-up. You give yourself away to please everybody else. You don't even know what you want, you've worked so hard to make them happy." I defended myself as Gena. "My survival depended on making them happy."

"Yes, but you keep doing it." I whined, "I don't know what else to do."

Gena shook her finger at me to punctuate her word, "Stand up for yourself. Tell the truth. Ask for what you want." I whimpered, "I can't."

"Don't do that," Gena raised her voice. "I hate it when you act like a victim." "I'll do whatever you want," I placated her.

"Jesse, stop it! You're playing me too well." Gena laughed. "I just want you to like me."

"I do like you." Gena touched my knee. "In spite of all the ways I give myself away?" "I want you to stop giving yourself away," Gena commanded.

"Would you be willing to take yourself back?" asked Vince. "I don't want to be that person," Gena hesitated. "Okay, I take myself back," she whispered, hiding her face in her hands sobbing. When she lowered her hands, we saw a new expression.

"Could you care about someone like you and me?" I asked. "It's easier if it's you," Gena smiled.

"What advice do you have for people like us?" I asked. Gena answered. "Don't worry about all those other people. Go out there and say what you mean."

"Gena, what are you doing right now?" Vince asked. "Speaking my truth."

I asked her how she felt. "I feel good."

"How's your energy?" asked Vince. "Right now my energy is high. My head is clear."

"I think you're being pretty hard on Jesse. She's actually a very nice person," teased Vince. "But I like this clear, powerful, wise woman over here even better." Vince touched Gena's arm as he complimented her. "She's terrific." Casey said, "I'm impressed, where have you been hiding this powerhouse? I want to see more of the real you."

Gena said, "This is different. This is really different. I feel really good. I didn't think it would work. I was just going to play along, but I'm in a new place. I like it. Can I keep this?" Gena asked. "Probably not," said Vince. "But you can find it again. I think you just released a black hole."

Gena's charming pirate pattern had been in control. By exploring, understanding, and accepting her pattern of pleasing others she released her black hole. A lifetime of running this pattern ensures that she will encounter it again, but now she recognizes it and has a choice. She can fall into that familiar black hole or change her behavior.

The energy field created by the open, accepting attention of Vince and Casey allowed Gena to experience herself from a new vantage point. Without this energy field, Gena would not have been able to see herself with compassion and acceptance.

Gena released her black hole by accepting what she didn't like about herself. Black holes that have been released may be triggered again, but less often and less intensely. Once we have released the energy of a black hole, we can change our automatic reaction.

——————— • • • • • ———————

I'd like to share two processes that you can use to explore and release your black holes. Working with my clients and colleagues has helped me develop these processes, but my most intimate experiences with black holes have been my own. We are only beginning to understand how to explore and release black holes. I've learned that knowing the release process and teaching it to others is the easy part. Releasing our own black holes is the hard part.

Sometimes when I release a black hole it seems to be permanently erased and isn't triggered again. More commonly my released black holes return, at least for a while. Exploring a new black hole is usually confounding and intense for me. It is much easier to explore and release the second time. By giving each significant black hole a name, such as "feeling abandoned," "feeling rejected," "fear of failure," or "feeling inadequate," I can recognize it more easily the next time. Some of my black holes will be with me for life. The best I can hope for is to recognize them and change my reaction.

When we catch ourselves in a black hole, we do have choices, even though we may feel stuck. We can notice our reaction, make a mental note of what triggered it, and then explore and release it later, or we can explore and release the black hole when it is triggered. Some of us are ready to create the time and resources to launch an intensive program of finding and releasing black holes. Others want to develop more support before facing a black hole. Still others turn to professional therapists for assistance. Decide what you are ready for and how much support you need. Even if you do not have time available or friends to help you, this book can give you an awareness of the process.

We have still another choice, to break our normal pattern and react differently the moment a black hole gets triggered, without doing the deeper work of discovering what's in the black hole at that time. If you usually get quiet and withdrawn when one of your black holes is triggered, keep talking and ask for help. If you usually raise your voice in anger, ask for some time to yourself. If you usually try to explain or justify your black hole reaction, say how you're feeling instead. Notice what happens when you change your reaction. Changing your reaction is different from avoidance and denial. When we change our reaction, we recognize the black hole as ours and consciously choose a different response. Staying out of our black holes is much easier after they have been explored and released. In denial, we don't realize that we are avoiding our black holes by reacting automatically. In denial, we usually react with a pirate pattern.

The most important ingredient for releasing black holes is an energy field of loving acceptance. If you can hold two realities in your awareness at the same time, you may be able to provide this for yourself. If you meditate regularly and have confidence in your ability to hold yourself in a state of grace while you are experiencing pain and fear, releasing black holes on your own is possible. If you don't have a regular practice of prayer and meditation, I would encourage you to find a couple of friends to hold an energy field of loving acceptance for you as you explore your tender memories and limiting beliefs.

Find two friends who accept and love you. That alone may be challenging, but remember that we are learning together how to change our lives. When we are vulnerable, we need friends who can listen and acknowledge our painful stories. If instead they join us in humiliation, blame, or disgust, we are on our own to release our black hole—a difficult task. I cannot overemphasize the powerful effect of friends' loving energy in the releasing process. When we are in the vulnerable state of experiencing our black holes, our friends' emotions, beliefs, and intentions dominate our merged energy fields.

Invite only friends who can be trusted to put their pirate strategies away. We open vulnerable memories as we explore and release our black holes. It is dangerous to explore them when we don't feel safe. Loving, accepting energy is essential to guide us through the release point.

Friends provide loving energy when they listen and accept what we have to say. Love can be expressed by sitting quietly and patiently waiting for what happens next. Love has no preconceived notions; it does not lead or redirect. Love is patient and kind; it doesn't judge or blame. Love surrenders control to an expansive spiritual energy field. Loving energy accommodates everything that happens with acceptance. Different from the energy of black holes, loving energy doesn't need protection. Love connects; it does not close off or shut down, even in pain. Love is always accepting. Acceptance explores with reverent curiosity. Loving acceptance is sometimes quiet, sometimes curious, always open and flowing.

Loving friends accept whatever we have done and see from a higher perspective that we can do no wrong. It is much easier to offer loving acceptance once our black holes have been released. Black holes clog the flow of loving energy.

Choose friends who have done some of their own personal work to release black holes. Friends are usually a better choice than family members. Families often have tangled black holes and unconscious pirate patterns. One black hole reaction can easily trigger another. A support person struggling with his own feelings of shame and fear has a hard time holding a loving energy field. Some committed partners have learned to help each other release their black holes, however.

I have designed two black hole release processes. As a starting place for both processes, I recommend a quiet space to reflect and learn from your experience, spiritual guides to call on, and caring friends with compassionate listening skills. Black holes are usually triggered automatically, but you can also intentionally trigger a black hole. Either way, the beginning step is to create a field of loving acceptance.

The first process is mind-centered. We can mentally explore and accept painful emotional experiences. Good therapists use variations of the mind-centered process. When we experience the vulnerable center of our black holes—our fear, shame, or sense of inadequacy—we can gain a new perspective on what happened. Our view of what happened shifts from vulnerability to greater understanding. New information is available to help us change our beliefs, and release tender emotional memories.

The second process is body-centered. Physical sensations such as tension and discomfort can help us experience black holes and notice where they manifest in our bodies. We can experience a physical sense of our hidden vulnerabilities. Focused breathing and physical movement can release emotional energy from our black holes. Black holes can be released physically and emotionally even when we don't understand them mentally.

If life were a river, black holes would be the rapids. In sea kayaking and canoeing, the excitement of white water can be terrifying at the beginning, but thrilling and energizing after a successful run. Getting in and out of black holes is similar because we are traveling through challenging and unfamiliar territory. Not everyone enjoys running rivers, and not everyone is willing to explore their black holes.

In kayaking, my friends and I don't go out in stormy or threatening weather or with people who aren't safe. We wait for a warm sunny day when we have plenty of time. Similarly, when you explore a black hole, choose your company carefully and set aside enough time to fully explore your hidden emotional memories. Be prepared to feel a little anxious as you head into a black hole. When we swamp a boat in the middle of the rapids, we need additional time and more help. Getting lost in a black hole also requires more time and help.

We choose a river with interesting, but not suicidal rapids. Start with simple black holes to develop your skill and trust in your friends. White water, like black holes, can be rough and dangerous, if we are not prepared. My friends and I learned river skills before we ran the Colorado River through the Grand Canyon. Reading rivers, knowing how to find the safest path through the rapids, gave us a mental map for what to look for and how to proceed. This chapter gives you a mental map for how to explore black holes. When you develop skill in releasing smaller black holes, you are ready to take on more challenging ones.

Choose the waters well and prepare your friends to help you through. When you are swept successfully into the calm water below the rapids, you will feel a burst of energy—a rush. Exhilaration is another reward for releasing black holes.

To begin, choose one black hole to explore. You may already know of several. However, knowing that you have a black hole is as different from experiencing the secret memories stored in it as reading a play is from playing the leading role. We may know that criticism triggers our defensive reactions. We can think about our past reactions and understand that this happens. Knowing this doesn't keep it from happening, though. In releasing a black hole, we experience the tender emotions and physical sensations hidden deep in it. A black hole can't be released until we fully experience and accept what was hidden.

We experience a black hole on four levels—mental, emotional, physical, and spiritual. We experience mental understanding and deeply held decisions and beliefs. We experience vulnerable protected emotions such as terror, humiliation, rejection, and confusion. We experience sensations such as discomfort, tension, throbbing, flushing, and dizziness. We may also experience a field of spiritual grace or acceptance for human mistakes and frailties. When a black hole is released, at least three of the four levels are fully engaged. Simultaneously experiencing our mental understanding, our physical sensations, our vulnerable emotions, and spiritual acceptance aligns our energy fields for release.

It is not enough to do physical movement, or massage. It is not enough to feel vulnerable and weep. It is not enough to talk out our understanding. It is not enough to meditate and pray. Black holes are released when all four levels are experienced together.

To begin, look for the key black hole indicators—emotional intensity, critical judgment, physical discomfort, and spiritual disconnection. Perhaps you feel guilty or ashamed about something trivial. Feeling terrible about having hurt someone's feelings can be a black hole. You may notice your judgment or desire for someone to change. You may be aware of blaming someone. Energy pirating may be able to help you find your black holes. If you notice that there is someone you avoid, ask yourself why. Fear and anxiety are excellent signposts to black holes. Following any of these indicators will help you find your black holes.

MIND-CENTERED BLACK HOLE RELEASE PROCESS

As I discussed above, black holes entangle four levels of our experience: our physical sensations, our mental understanding, our emotional reactions, and our spiritual essence. In the mind-centered release process, our mental understanding leads, but the other three are involved. This process begins when a black hole is triggered, either automatically or on purpose. The process helps us find a story that we understand from the more vulnerable perspective of our childhood. There are questions that help us explore our stories and compare our emotional memories with what we know now as adults. Our adult perspective provides new information that allows us to expand our understanding and accept our emotional and physical sensations. When our personal stories are experienced and witnessed with acceptance, our black holes are released. By exploring our emotional memories, at the least, we reduce the intensity of our black hole reactions.

Intentionally triggering a black hole can get you started in the mind-centered release process. Invite the friends you have chosen to support you to invent a role-play scenario to trigger your black hole. For example, if feeling controlled triggers your black hole, they can pretend to control you. If people who discount you trigger your black hole, they can pretend to ignore and exclude you.

Choose a black hole and describe in detail what triggers it. Your friends may want to ask questions to understand exactly how to trigger your black hole. Be sure to get your friends' agreement that when your black hole has been triggered, they will stop role-playing and switch to loving support.

Once everyone has agreed to the process, leave the room so they can plan how to trigger your black hole. Have one of them call you back when they are ready. Leave it up to them to decide how to begin. Let them know when your black hole has been triggered, so they can then provide loving support.

When your black hole has been triggered, allow your hidden emotions, sensations, and beliefs to wash over you like a hot shower. Experience your reactions, and at the same time observe yourself reacting. You will develop a double awareness: one, experiencing your physical sensations and emotions; two, observing and understanding what is happening to you. The observer is your spiritual self, aware and accepting of all that is happening, while your physical self courageously experiences the discomfort of your black hole. Your observer self is like an outrigger on a canoe. Without the wide arm of the outrigger stabilizing the canoe, it would roll over and sink in the waves. The outrigger steadies the canoe in rough water. Our spiritual observer-self steadies us during troubling experiences.

Double awareness is a high-level skill. It may take some practice. Meditation strengthens your observer-self and your ability to notice your emotional and physical sensations. Your observer-self can help guide you through the release process. Allow your experience to unfold as you notice and explore. If you get lost in your emotions or frightened by them, focus on your breath. Notice yourself breathing in and then out. Your observer-self is the one who notices your breathing.

If you have invited friends to help you explore and release your black holes, walk your friends through the following seven-step release process, and encourage them to read Chapter 7, Listening and Reflecting Energy, before you start.

The loving acceptance of your friends is one way that spiritual acceptance is present in the release process. Another form of spiritual support is your observer-self noticing and accepting your experiences. A third way to bring spiritual support into the process is to ask for it outright. Before you explore a black hole, say a short prayer stating your intention to release a black hole and asking for support from your spiritual source. I believe that we each have guardian angles and spiritual guides that help us with life's difficulties. If you are aware of your guides, speak to them directly. Spiritual support can come from many different religious and spiritual traditions. Choose words from your own religious practice that are meaningful to you. If you don't have a spiritual tradition, here is one way to request spiritual support.

> *Deepest Wisdom, Highest Guidance, we invite our life force and source energies to help us create a loving, accepting energy field for the purpose of exploring and releasing black holes. We invite the energies of our guides and angels to help us access all levels of wisdom. We do this in the service of healing, evolving, true learning, and the highest good of all concerned.*

Asking for spiritual assistance helps maintain a loving energy field. Use what brings you the most comfort.

Seven Steps of the Mind-Centered Release Process

The seven steps below can serve as a guide for the mind-centered release process. You may find that you don't use all the steps or that you naturally invent additional steps. There is no magic to the steps. The magic is in the release point—experiencing tender, hidden emotions and witnessing yourself in that experience within a field of loving acceptance. The steps help you find the release point and create a loving energy field. Once you have triggered your black hole, follow the steps that seem helpful.

1. *Notice* that you are in a black hole.
2. *Claim* it as a black hole and take ownership of this familiar experience.
3. *Explore* the emotions, beliefs, and sensations hidden in your black hole.
4. *Expand* your understanding by comparing your black hole experience with your current experience.
5. *Discover* what you want as a result of your new understanding.
6. *Test* the trigger to find out if your black hole has been released.
7. *Name* the black hole so you will recognize it if it triggers again.

Step 1. Notice that you are in a black hole.
Breathe slowly and fully as you begin to feel vulnerable emotions and sensations. Noticing your breathing moves your awareness into your observer-self. Let your friends know when your black hole has been triggered so they can offer loving acceptance. Friends who remain open to everything that happens in this process and who accept your experience give you the best chance of releasing your black hole. Friends who join you in blame and outrage keep your black hole from releasing.

*n it as a black hole and take ownership of this familiar
'ence.*

_gnize that your vulnerable emotions are your black hole. At this point, your friends can ask questions to help you define your internal experience. Using their own best judgment, they can also ask other questions that might help: Are you in a black hole? What are you experiencing? What are you noticing? Where are you feeling a reaction in your body? What does it feel like?

Close your eyes and answer each question thoughtfully. Take time to observe your thoughts and feelings. Notice whether these sensations and emotions are familiar to you. Continue to be aware of your breathing. As you breathe into tender emotions, your breath begins to move the energy. Breathe in and out with conscious awareness.

*Step 3. Explore the emotions, beliefs, and sensations hidden in your
black hole.*

Allow your mind to wander back to earlier experiences that felt similar to what you are experiencing. Let curiosity lead you to your most vulnerable emotions. Then open your experience to the loving energy field around you. Your friends can ask questions like the following to help you find the story and learn more about your black hole: When did you feel this way before? What is your earliest memory of feeling this way? What is happening? How old are you? Where are you? Who else is there? What are you doing? What do you see? What do you hear people saying? How are you feeling?

Respond to your friends' questions and reflect on your findings. You may not notice much at first. Be patient with yourself and allow your mind to respond to each question. Answer with what comes to mind. Your story may begin to take shape. Your emotions may grow stronger. Remember to breathe. You may experience pain, sorrow, shame, or anger. You may want to cry. Crying can be an effective release for black holes. Allow your feelings and your tears to flow. Don't try to stop them or change them.

Step 4. Expand your understanding by comparing your black hole experience with your current experience.

This step involves two perspectives—one from the past and the current one. Holding both of these perspectives allows your past perspective to merge with the present and release your black hole. The questions your friends ask in this step call on your observer-self: How is today similar to the past? How is today different from the past? How are you different now than you were then?

Try to be aware of both your observer-self seeing you as you are today and your black hole experience simultaneously. Compare your two experiences by answering your friends' questions. As you compare these two experiences in the presence of your friends' loving energy, your black hole experience begins to shift. You may gain a new understanding of your personal story. You can expect to feel your emotions and sensations lighten and release as you open these two perspectives to each other. You are creating one aligned energy field from two perspectives that have been unaware of each other.

Step 5. Discover what you want as a result of your new understanding.

Moving from your vulnerable experience to what you want pulls you out of your black hole. Your friends can help you develop a plan for what to do with what you've learned. By having a plan, you are more likely to avoid your black hole in the future. Your friends can help by asking questions to help you plan: What do you want in the present situation? What can you do to create that outcome? How can we help you do that? What do you want to do differently in the future?

Step 6. Test the trigger to find out if your black hole has been released.

If you feel peaceful and complete, and your energy has returned, you can test the trigger for your black hole. Plan a new response to your black hole. Have your friends replay the triggering scenario. Respond in the new way. Notice the difference.

*Step 7. Name the black hole so you will recognize it if it triggers
      again.*

The final step is to name your black hole. A name is a shorthand way
of recognizing it. Eventually, you will be able to notice when it is
triggered and say to yourself, "Oh yes, this is my 'needs approval'
black hole," or my "feeling inadequate" black hole, or my "hates
criticism" black hole. Adding the phrase "I do that sometimes," can
help you avoid your black hole. Its name becomes a way to stay out
of it. With a little practice, you will no longer react to that black
hole. The following stories illustrate the mind-centered release
process and will help you understand more about how to do it.

——————— · · · · · ———————

My colleagues Chris and Les met at my home one Saturday in April.
We sat in wooden chairs around my dining room table. I asked them
to help me release my fear of rejection.

Chris and Les asked me questions to learn more about exactly
what seemed to trigger my black hole. They agreed to invent a
scenario that would exclude me. I went downstairs while Chris and
Les planned a conversation that would trigger my black hole. They
decided not to call me back as a way to begin the role-play.

After a while I called up from downstairs, "Are you ready yet?"
Chris and Les ignored me. "Okay, I get it," I said, as I returned
upstairs.

When I sat down, Chris and Les were talking about a training
program they were planning. It was a program for my favorite
corporate client. By the time Chris and Les agreed that they didn't
need anyone else for the program, I was hooked. My black hole was
triggered. I felt vulnerable, uneasy, hot, embarrassed. (*Notice it*)

I breathed into the sinking sensation in my stomach by
imagining that each breath was flowing into my belly. I felt rejected,
not good enough, not wanted. Chris checked in with me. "Have you
found your black hole?" "Yes." (*Claim it*)

Chris and Les stopped role-playing and switched to loving
acceptance. "Where are you feeling a reaction in your body?" asked
Les. "Here, in my stomach." I folded my arms around my waist.

"What does it feel like?" asked Les. "Nauseous, tense," I said, squeezing my arms in tight.

"When have you felt this way before?" asked Chris. "I don't know."

"Do you get any fragments or pictures?" Les encouraged. I closed my eyes. "There's a door....It's the door to my brothers' room....It's closed." (*Explore it*)

"What's happening on the other side of the door?" asked Chris. "When I was a kid, my brothers locked their bedroom door and pretended to have a great time without me. I'm standing outside the door yelling for them to let me in, but they won't."

"How old are you?" Les asked. "I'm seven. We just moved out of the nursery upstairs because my baby sister was born. We were all in the same big room together then. Now the boys have their own room and they've closed me out."

"How is today similar to the past?" Chris asked. "The two of you are leaving me out," I murmured.

"How is it different from the past?" Les asked. "You're helping by asking questions," I whispered.

"How are you different?" Les inquired. I straightened up in my chair. "I've grown up. I know how to take care of myself. I have other friends," I said a little defensively. (*Expand it*)

"What do you want now?" Chris asked. I opened my eyes. "I want to be included. I want to be loved. I want my contribution to be valued." (*Move beyond it*)

"What can you do to get what you want?" asked Chris. "I can ask you if you love me," I said. "I love the socks off you, my dear friend," said Chris. Les said, "I love you, too." "You remember that time you taught my class when I was so sick. What would I do without a good friend like you?" "It's amazing, I hear what you're saying in a different way. It's landing in a new place inside me. I believe you. I'm feeling warm and comfortable." (*Release point*)

"What else can you do?" asked Chris. "I can ask you how you're going to do this program for my client without me." I laughed. "You know you can't do it without me."

"We know that, but let's test you," said Chris. "Are you ready for a test?" asked Les. "I think so. Something has shifted. My energy is back. Give it a try." (*Test it*)

Chris and Les resumed talking about the training program and how they would split up the work. "You guys can't even begin to do this program without me," I cut in, laughing. "I can't believe you'd even want to talk about it without me."

"That's a new response," said Chris. "Yeah, I like it. How are you feeling?" Les asked. "It's gone. I'm feeling different. Something has shifted. You really had me going at first, but now it feels easy. The key was feeling your love."

"Do you want to name this black hole?" asked Les. "It's my rejection black hole," I said. (*Name it*)

——————— • • • • • ———————

My brothers and I had been close; that shifted, and I hadn't grieved the loss. I had hidden my sorrow in a black hole. Once I exposed the inner sanctum of my black hole, the loving energy of Les and Chris flowed into it. My black hole was released, my core belief shifted, and my energy became balanced. My rejection black hole was released easily. The whole process took about an hour. Most black holes actually release in a few minutes, but time is required to find the release point and balance our energy afterward. I have revisited this black hole several times since and found other rejection stories, but none so painful as the first time.

Your own story may be so painful that you have trouble opening it. It may help to know that no one version of a story is fully correct. When witnesses testify in court, they all tell slightly different stories. Assume that there is more to your story than you can remember. When you feel the vulnerable center of your black hole, tell yourself a different story. This is creative storytelling. Make up a version of the story the way you would have wanted it. Tell both the old story and a new story. Expand the possibilities of what might have happened. The old story doesn't go away, but the emotional energy it contained can be released through the possibility of a different story.

For example, I could have expanded my story by inventing a new reason for my brothers' behavior. Perhaps they teased me because they liked me. Perhaps my older brother was jealous that my younger brother and I were close. Perhaps I had done something to my brothers and they were retaliating. Any of these creative stories could have been true. The key is to expand your perception beyond the story that is stuck in the past at the same moment that you are fully experiencing the emotions and sensations enmeshed in the story. Here is a mind-centered release story.

—————— · · · · · ——————

Jon, a medical doctor, is very calm, an attribute that is just right for the emergency room where he works. Jon and his wife, Sharon, came to work with me to explore and release their black holes. A couple of their friends, Carol and Peter, joined us.

Jon volunteered to be first to explore a black hole. Jon claimed criticism as one of his triggers. Sharon and Carol volunteered to trigger Jon's black hole while Peter agreed to support Jon. Jon left the room.

The group decided that his wife Sharon would play herself and Carol would pretend to be a dissatisfied medical patient. Once they agreed on the plot, Peter went to get Jon. When Jon sat down in the group, Sharon accused him of leaving his work tools—electric drill and screwdrivers—by the front door of their home. She also claimed that he forgot to clean up after the dog and was late getting home. Carol complained that she was in pain all the time because the medicine Jon gave her wasn't working. It didn't take much of this for Jon to find his black hole.

"Have you felt this way before?" Carol asked. "Every time I'm criticized," said Jon. (*Claim it*)

"When you were a kid did you feel this way?" Sharon asked. "Yes," Jon confessed.

"What was happening then?" Sharon inquired. "My mother was criticizing me." (*Explore it*)

"It must have hurt when your mother didn't like what you did," Carol commented. Jon nodded. "My mother criticized my dad a lot and she told me never to be like him."

"She didn't want you to be like your dad," Carol reflected. "No. She thought he was good for nothing and criticized him all the time," said Jon.

"So you didn't want to be like him," acknowledged Sharon. "No, and every time I'm criticized I'm afraid I won't be loved," admitted Jon.

"How does that feel?" Carol asked. John folded his arms, bowed his head, and mumbled, "Terrible...lost...scared...alone."

"Can you feel that now?" inquired Sharon. Jon, his head sinking lower, said yes.

"Where do you feel it?" Sharon asked. Jon rubbed his chest. "Here, in my heart."

They waited while Jon breathed into the pain in his chest. "How are you different now from when you were a kid?" Carol asked. John shook his head. "I don't know."

"Does Sharon love you?" asked Carol. John looked up slowly. "I hope so." (*Expand it*)

Sharon leaned forward. "Jon, I want you to know that I love you very deeply." "Even when I leave my electric drill by the front door?" "Yes, even when you leave your tools in the house, I love you."

"How is the current situation different from the past?" Carol asked. "Sharon loves me." Jon's eyes crinkled with tiny smile lines. (*Release point*)

"I do, and you are not your dad." Sharon looked directly into his eyes. "No, I'm not my dad, and you love me even if I'm not perfect."

"Jon, what do you want?" asked Peter. "I want to know that I'm loved." Sharon took Jon's hands, pulled him to his feet, and held him close.

"Now how do you feel?" asked Carol. "I'm feeling much better." Jon grinned.

"How's your energy?" Peter inquired. "Good, I'm feeling really good." He rocked Sharon from side to side.

"Are you ready for a test?" asked Carol. "Yes, I'm ready." Jon and Sharon sat down.

"Jon, why did you let the dog in with all that mud? I've been waiting for you to get home and now there's all this mud to clean up," Sharon accused. Jon grinned. (*Test it*)

"I'm really not feeling well. This prescription you gave me isn't working. You must not be a very good doctor," said Carol. "Tell me more about how you're feeling," Jon said evenly.

"I've been throwing up ever since you gave me this," Carol complained. "Let's get that taken care of for you," said Jon.

"How are you doing, Jon?" Peter asked. "I feel different. I think the black hole is gone. I was afraid of being like my dad and how my mom treated him. I didn't ever want to be treated that way. I didn't realize...what a relief. You've helped me with a big change."

Black holes don't usually leave immediately, but they can fade away. Each time we own them and change our reaction, they have less power. Jon still doesn't like to be criticized, but sooner or later he catches himself and changes his reaction. Now, when he feels criticized, he can say, "I'm feeling criticized right now and I'm getting that old feeling to shut down and go away. But I know that you love me, even though I may have made a mistake. So let's talk." When Jon changed his pattern, Sharon's pattern shifted also. They find talking about problems easier now.

——— · · · · · ———

BODY-CENTERED BLACK HOLE RELEASE PROCESS

The body-centered release of black holes involves finding and releasing energy blocks through movement and awareness of your physical sensations. Emotional experience, mental understanding, and spiritual acceptance all play a role, but physical sensations lead the process. Some black holes are more easily released through the body-centered process; and some people are more comfortable focusing on their physical rather than mental awareness.

Body-centered release works best with fears that we experience physically—tension, nausea, racing heart, etc. In this process, we physically explore the sensations created by our fears, and the humiliation and frustration that accompanies these fears. As some of our anxiety is released, deeper fears may emerge. The body-centered process explores layers of anxiety until no other fears surface. There is usually a positive purpose at the root of our fears.

Our fears have protected us in our lives. A valuable part of this process is to find the original positive purpose of our fears.

As in the mind-centered release process, black holes can be triggered automatically or intentionally. Once your black hole has been triggered, you will notice tightness or discomfort in your body. By focusing on your physical sensations, you can reach the vulnerable inner sanctum of your black hole. Physical movement provides the energy to expand and release black holes. Conscious breathing alone can release physical sensations and emotions.

While the mind-centered release process expands the story connected to the black hole, the body-centered release process expands the associated physical sensations. Both explore the vulnerable emotions that are protected by your black hole, and both use conscious breathing for energy release. The mind-centered release process focuses on expanding your understanding, while the body-centered releases focus on moving your physical sensations.

Five Steps of the Body-Centered Release Process

The five steps below can serve as a guide for the body-centered release process. You may not use all the steps or you may naturally find other steps that are more helpful. The release point is when you experience the most vulnerable inner sanctum of your black hole in a field of loving acceptance.

1. *Allow* fear to lead you into a black hole.
2. *Explore* and describe your physical sensations.
3. *Name* other hidden emotions.
4. *Expand* your physical sensations through conscious breathing and physical movement.
5. *Find* the lessons learned.

You can work with body-centered releases on your own or with the support of friends. If you work alone, your observer-self will need to provide a field of acceptance and grace. If you invite friends to help you, encourage them to read Chapter 7, Listening and Reflecting Energy, before you start. I also recommend asking for spiritual support and guidance.

1. Allow fear to lead you into a black hole.

There are two ways to find your fears in order to get started with body-centered release. The easiest way to start is to name something you are afraid of—illness, failure, public speaking, loneliness, dying alone, feeling out of control. Ask yourself where you feel this fear in your body. Notice any tightness, discomfort, tingling, or other sensations. Another way to find fear is to notice a persistent pattern—an illness, an addiction, a repeating thought pattern, a pirating pattern. Look for something in your life that is not working, something that seems to have a pattern or a life of its own. Explore how this pattern serves you, how it limits you, and what the pattern is most afraid to admit. Answer each question thoughtfully. Notice where you feel the fear in your body. These are some of the questions that can be helpful in finding fear:

- What are you afraid of? (If this answer is clear, skip to step 2.)
- What are you struggling with?
- How does this pattern serve you?
- How does this pattern limit you?
- What is this pattern most afraid to admit?

2. Explore and describe your physical sensations.

Once fear has triggered a black hole, focus on your physical reaction. Surrender to the experience. No need to say anything while you get accustomed to your feelings. Notice your reaction and consciously breathe into the physical sensations. Imagine your breath flowing into your tension and discomfort. Experience both physical sensations and emotions as you breathe.

Describe where in your body you are feeling a reaction. The most common areas are heart, belly, head, and throat, but you may feel tension or discomfort almost anywhere. Describe the sensation to your friends as though you can see it. What color is it—black, gray, yellow? What consistency is it—hard like metal, gooey like phlegm? What does it remind you of—rags, wood, steel bands, crumpled paper? The description helps you acknowledge your blocked energy. The following questions can help you describe your physical reaction:

- Where do you feel the fear in your body?
- What does it feel like?
- What does it look like?
- What color is it?
- What does it remind you of?

3. *Name other hidden emotions.*

You may feel tightness in your belly, tension in your lower back, heaviness in your heart. Name each significant sensation and consciously breathe into it until it eases. Ask yourself or have your friends ask you questions like these:

- What would be even worse than [the original fear]—more frightening, more humiliating, more troubling?
- Where is this new feeling located in your body?
- Is there any shame, anger, or frustration associated with your fear?
- Who are you angry or frustrated with?
- Is there anyone else that you are frustrated or angry with?
- Where is that frustration (shame or anger) located in your body?
- What does it look and feel like?
- Is there anything that would be worse?

(Repeat the list of questions until there is nothing worse.)

4. *Expand your physical sensations through conscious breathing and physical movement.*

As you explore your black hole, focus on breathing. Your breath can move energy. As you breathe into your physical sensations, your breathing releases energy. Think of your breath like bellows for an emotional fire. Your breath will fan the flames of your emotions so that you can fully experience your black hole. Think of your emotion as fuel. Eventually, the emotional fire dies out as the fuel is consumed. Surrender to your pain. Accept your fear. Willingly be in a vulnerable, emotional place. You are surviving whatever was hidden. Getting out of a black hole can take from a few minutes to several hours depending on how much fuel you have to burn. As your fire cools, your energy will rise.

When there is no more to be afraid of, imagine that you are removing all the energy sensations that you have described. Hold the firm intention to remove the blocked energy. You can move your arms to brush off the energy or imagine yourself pulling blocked energy out of your body. Imagine stripping invisible energy off and piling it on the floor. Describe the imaginary pile. What color is it, what consistency?

Instead of imagining yourself removing blocked energy, you may want to walk, dance, run, play sports, or move your body rhythmically to release the energy. Only move in ways that feel safe. Any safe movement will help. If you believe that what you are doing will release your blocked energy, it will.

When you have released your black hole, your physical sensations will lessen. They may not completely disappear, but they will feel more comfortable than during steps two and three. Sometimes the complete release of physical sensations requires a few weeks, just as physical healing from an injury can take several weeks. Black holes may need additional time for complete release and healing.

5. Find the lessons learned.

Once your physical sensations lighten, you may want to clarify what you have learned from the release process. Ask the imaginary pile of blocked energy what messages it has for you, or simply ask yourself what you have learned. What message does the blocked energy have for you? Notice whatever comes into your mind and write it down or tell your friends. If nothing occurs to you, that's fine too. These questions can be helpful in avoiding this particular black hole in the future, but may not be necessary.

The body-centered release is a slower process than the mind-centered release. You will need a minute or two to breathe into each experience triggered by the questions in the steps above. As you consider each question and breathe into the feeling in your body, each new sensation will expand and then release. Eventually you will find nothing else more frightening or humiliating. Your sensations and emotions will have lessened.

As you do this work make no assumptions about what is the best outcome for you. Recognize that wherever you go is the right place for you to be. If you feel off track, go further along that line. Don't assume that you know what might be next or how you are supposed to feel. Follow your body and trust your spiritual and human guides. Whenever you feel stuck and don't know what to do, breathe into and explore your physical sensations. Some people gain insight by asking their spiritual guides to access deeper wisdom.

As with the mind-centered process, the body-centered release process works best in the presence of loving acceptance. Once you begin the journey to release a black hole, you will find it difficult to turn back. Stopping part way can increase your anxiety, like getting caught in the middle of rapids on a river. Going all the way through a black hole—exploring and expanding your pattern—will release it. If you get stuck, almost any movement will help release a black hole. The more free-flowing the activity the more release you experience. This is one of the reasons people move around physically when they are frustrated or angry. They walk away, throw things, or slam doors. I do not recommend these actions, but people naturally do them to release energy.

You may want to develop some physical energy release exercises. For example, many men enjoy competitive sports for the physical movement and emotional release it provides. Women seem to enjoy dancing and aerobic movement classes. My personal choice of movement is running. After 25 years of running, I am no longer surprised that I have more energy after running than before.

In addition to physical movement, black holes can be released through therapeutic treatment of your physical body, as in physical therapy, chiropractic adjustments, acupuncture, massage, cranial-sacral work, and guided breathing. There are also energy practitioners who work with and move emotional energy.

Additional techniques can help if you get stuck in the process of releasing a black hole.

——————— · · · · · ———————

My colleague Jerry asked me to help him release a black hole he had about his work. Jerry consults with Fortune 500 companies, working with up to a hundred people at a time. I sat in his office as we talked about his fears.

"I know I'm good at what I do," Jerry said. "I've been doing it for years. Everyone tells me they like my work. I don't know why I get so anxious about it. It doesn't make any sense." "I've watched you work with people. The honesty and insight you bring is masterful."

"I'm so fortunate to have this office. My wife and I just remodeled it to let the garden in." Jerry twitched his pencil. "You did a great job. It's so peaceful in here with all the flowers and light."

"It is peaceful. That's ironic, you know. I feel so anxious about my first assignment with this new client. I can't settle down and just enjoy being here in my new office." Jerry perched on the edge of his chair. "Would you like to explore what that's about?" I offered.

Jerry said he would and I asked, "Would you mind if I ask for some guidance for this process?" "No, I don't mind, maybe it will help." I closed my eyes. "Deepest Wisdom, I ask for your guidance and help as we explore Jerry's anxiety. I invite source energies along with Jerry's guides and angels to participate with us for the healing and highest good of all concerned."

I asked Jerry what he was anxious about. "I was hired by a national consulting firm to learn their programs and I did—no problem. But now I'm doing their three-day training program for the first time and it's with a client I've never worked with before." (*Find the fear*)

"And it makes you nervous." "Yeah. I'm really feeling anxious about it. I'm afraid I'll screw up just because I'm nervous. I know the material. I've delivered stuff like this for years, but I'm afraid that I'll try so hard to be really good that it will come across as me trying rather than me being genuinely me. I'm afraid I'll try so hard to do it right that I won't make it my own. Does that make any sense?"

"Yes, it does makes sense. Where in your body do you feel the anxiety?" "Here." Jerry placed his hand on his chest.

"You feel it in your heart? What is the sensation like in your heart?" I asked. "It's a tightness with a fluttery feeling behind the tightness." (Explore it)

"Let yourself just be with your fear. Let the anxiety tighten." Jerry closes his eyes. I waited. "Now it's moved," he announced.

"Where is it now?" I asked. "Here." Jerry moved his hand a little lower, over his solar plexus.

"What is the sensation there?" I asked quietly. "Discomfort, it feels like pressure, it's not fluttering anymore."

"Think about the presentation you will be giving next week and see the people responding to you. Be with that pressure, the anxiety, the feeling of discomfort," I suggested. Jerry sat motionless, but for his breathing. "Okay, it's lessening now. The pressure has let up a little."

"What would be even worse than trying too hard and not being yourself in front of people?" I asked. "They wouldn't like me. They'd hate me. They wouldn't ask me back. I'd feel like a failure." Jerry sagged in his chair. (Find other emotions)

"You'd feel like a failure, and they wouldn't want you back. Can you feel that sensation?" "Yes. I don't like it. It feels awful."

"Where do you feel it?" Jerry moved his hand back up his chest. "Here, it's back in my heart."

"What does it feel like?" "Constricted, my heart feels tight like there's a metal band around me."

"Your heart feels tight and you feel like a failure," I acknowledged. Jerry shifted in his chair, his eyes still closed.

"What would be even worse than being a failure? What would be even worse than people hating you?" I asked quietly. "I'd be ostracized from society. No one would want me. They'd tell me to go away. I'd have to leave. I wouldn't know how to survive. I'd die. That would be worse than being a failure. I'd be dead." Jerry's chin quivered.

"Does that make you angry?" "Yeah, actually, I'm more frustrated."

"Whom are you frustrated with?" "First it was with the group for not wanting me, but now I'm frustrated with me for trying so hard when all I have to do is go in and be myself. Why do I try so hard? I'm good just the way I am."

"You are good just the way you are, and you're frustrated with yourself for trying so hard," I said. "Where do you feel that?" Jerry ran his hand from his chest to his solar plexus. "All of this," he said slowly. "All of me."

"What does it feel like?" "It hurts inside, like something is gripping my insides, hurting me."

"Be with that feeling, the gripping, the hurting, the feeling that no one wants you and you try too hard, and you are dead." I waited for about two minutes, then asked, "Is there anything worse than that? Worse than no one wanting you and being dead?" "There is nothingness. I'm feeling nothingness now."

"How is that?" "It's not so bad, kind of pleasant actually. I'm just floating and it's peaceful. I'm okay." Almost imperceptibly, Jerry's eyebrows lifted.

"How are you feeling?" I asked. "The pressure is gone. The grip is less and getting better. I feel like I'm opening up a little." Jerry opened his eyes.

"I think you're ready for the next phase of the process." "What's that?"

"I want you to remove the anxiety, the fear of people hating you, ostracizing you. The frustration of trying too hard. I want you to pull it all off. Use your hands. Imagine it coming off. Do whatever you want to do to strip yourself of the anxiety, fear, and frustration." Jerry pulled at his chest and motioned toward the floor as if he were tearing off his shirt. He did the same with his solar plexus, throwing invisible fears on the floor. "There," he said, as he settled back into his chair. (*Expand it*)

"All off?" "There it is." He pointed to the floor off to the side.

"What does it look like in your mind's eye?" I asked. "Like clothes, old clothes that I don't need anymore."

"So it's okay to take them off." "Yeah, it feels good."

"There's just one more thing. I want you to ask the stuff on the floor what message it has for you. Every fear has a positive message and I want you to find out what the gift is." Jerry closed his eyes. "I can just be myself. I don't have to please anyone. I can genuinely be myself and that's okay, in fact it's good. That's really what they want anyway." Jerry grinned. (*Lessons learned*)

"And how are you doing?" I asked. "I'm feeling great—looser, freer, more open, lit up. This is a great process. I can't wait to work with this new client. I'm not worried about it at all. I'm eager to go. What a difference."

———— · · · · · ————

Barbara wanted to talk about her reaction to her daughter Molly's separation. She was struggling with the force of her desire to meddle in Molly's life. I asked her where she felt the struggle in her body. "Here in my heart." She put a hand over her heart. (*Find the fear*)

"What does it feel like?" "It's painful." Barbara started to cry.

I sat with her while she allowed the pain in her heart. "What are you afraid of?" I asked gently. "I'm afraid Molly is going to be all alone, with no one to take care of her." Barbara was still crying. (*Explore it*)

"Can you see Molly with your eyes closed?" I asked. "No, I see another women, someone very young. I don't know her. She's crying."

"Where is she?" "She's lying next to the road. It's raining and very cold. She's going to have a baby." Barbara sobbed. "There is no one to take care of her. It seems like she's my daughter, and I couldn't find her until now."

I sat quietly with Barbara while she cried. "She's not moving. I think she's dying," Barbara said.

"Can you imagine someone coming to help her?" I asked. "No one comes," Barbara wailed.

I sat quietly. "Wait, there is someone," Barbara said. "He wants to help her. He's helping her up. She's getting up. It's very hard. He's carrying her. He's taking her to a house nearby. They're going to take care of her. All it takes is one person to help."

"What happened?" I asked. "She wasn't married and she got

pregnant. Her father was ashamed of her. He had the care of her, but he wouldn't. She needs his help. She to stay with her even though she is going to die anyway.

"Where do you feel the need to help?" I asked. "Here in my he.. I feel a strong need to help, here in my heart."

"What needs to happen?" I'm just going to put my arms around her and love her. That's all she needs is someone to love her. All the pregnant women need to be loved. It heals me to send my love no matter what the outcome." (*Find other emotions*)

"Can you allow that feeling in your heart?" I asked. Barbara breathed into her heart for a few minutes. She seemed calmer.

"Is there anything around your heart that needs to be brushed off or pulled away?" I asked. Barbara pulled handfuls of imagined energy from her chest and let it drop on the floor. (*Expand it*)

"Does the pile of energy on the floor have a message for you?" I asked. "My love doesn't change the outcome, but it heals the hurt in my heart. I can always give love no matter what happens. Love makes all the difference." (*Lessons learned*)

"How are you feeling?" "I think I'm okay."

"Where do stories like that come from?" asked Barbara. "I don't know. It may be an archetypal story, something we can all relate to. Perhaps it's a story about your mother or your grandmother or someone that you've been close to. Perhaps it's a story you read in a book when you were younger. I think it's possible that we have had past lives and that we may hold stories of past traumatic experiences in our bodies. There is no way to know. What I do know is that when a story has that much power, it causes us to react automatically in the same way as emotional memories we recognize do. The only way to release the effect these stories have on us is to remember and experience them as you just did. Then we can allow it to be just a story and not have to be afraid or react compulsively, as you wanted to with Molly."

"I don't know who that young woman was. I'm sure my mother never had a story like that. It seemed too real to have been something I read in a book. I've never before had an experience that seemed like a past life, but this was extremely strong in me. That must be what it was." Barbara added, "I do feel much better. My heart isn't hurting, and I don't feel so compelled to save Molly's marriage. I think she'll work things out for herself."

——————— • • • • • ———————

In body-centered release, you may or may not find a story, and it doesn't matter what the story is. Fully experiencing the primary emotions—fear, sadness, and anger—in your body and allowing yourself to accept the story and any sensations is what releases the black hole.

RELEASING A BLACK HOLE ON YOUR OWN

When a black hole has been automatically triggered, you can seize the opportunity and release it on your own. Find a comfortable space by yourself, and ask your guides and angels to help you. Since you are already engulfed in the experience, you won't need to find its trigger. When you notice your reaction—the physical sensations of fear, embarrassment, anger, humiliation—get comfortable and breathe slowly, deeply, and rhythmically. Fan the flames of your emotion with the bellows of your breath. Let your body follow your impulse to move around, hold yourself, or be still.

Watch and listen to your thoughts as though you have a TV in your mind. Let your mind flip from channel to channel, from a commercial to a program and back again. Don't try to choose any particular channel. Just watch and listen for where your mind will go. Say to yourself what you are noticing: fear, confusion, analyzing, lost, back to the story, etc. Take mental notes of what you notice. Try to name your emotions and the physical sensations you experience. Let your experiences flow. Don't try to focus your thoughts, or stop them. Welcome everything that comes. Let your TV mind run and pay attention. Attend to your breathing. Breathing moves your energy and helps you stay grounded while you experience your black hole. If you find yourself lost in mental chatter, say to yourself, "Lost in thought again."

Once you are fully in the grip of your black hole, begin to guide your thoughts with the questions in this chapter. Ask yourself what your friends would say to you now. Your mind will answer your questions. Listen to your mind. Notice the protections you want to use to free yourself from your black hole, such as cynicism, blame, or judgment. Be careful not to jettison out of your black hole by blaming your reaction on someone else. Notice especially how your feelings intensify and then ease.

Whether you lead with your mind or body doesn't matter. Notice and claim your reaction, find your anxiety and explore all your sensations and emotions. Ask for help from your guides and angels. Ask yourself when you have felt this way before. Allow your stories and experiences to flow. Expand beyond the myopia of your black hole experience. Notice how different you feel and what you have learned. Go through the steps that help the most.

———— · · · · · ————

The following story shows how I explored and released my betrayal black hole alone late one Sunday night. Most black holes are easier to release than this one. Most take less than two hours to release. This one took all night.

I drove home from the Oregon coast, exhausting my will power in the effort to stay awake. Home at 10p.m., I dragged myself across the living room and up two flights of stairs with my bags. Eager for a welcoming voice, I switched on the answering machine in my bedroom.

"It's important that I talk with you tonight. Call me," the voice said. My heart jumped into my throat. I wondered if I would always react this way to Don. It had been almost a year since our divorce, but I still ached every time I thought about him. We were supposed to meet the next morning. I became anxious about why he wanted me to call him tonight. I looked up his new number, picked up the phone, and dialed.

Don asked how our two grown kids were. He was glad to hear they were fine and asked if they would be home for Christmas. I told him yes, and asked if that was what he wanted to talk about.

"No, there's something else I wanted to tell you. I appreciate you calling back. I wanted you to hear it from me, not from someone else. You know I've been seeing Lara." "Yes, you told me," I said, my heart pounding in my ears.

"I've given Lara an engagement ring." His words reverberated through me as through a hollow drum. "I had a feeling while I was at the coast that you would be getting married soon," I said. "I know that's what you want. I appreciate you telling me."

"How did you know?" he asked. I ignored his question.

"When is the wedding?" "September."

I wanted off the phone.

"Do you still want to meet in the morning?" "Yes, I'll see you at eight," said Don. We hung up.

I stared through the window into the darkness, feeling frozen in time, rigid, blank. My breath came in little sucking spasms like hiccups. Bands tightened around my chest. I leaned on the desk. An urgency grew within me to dash for the toilet bowl around the corner. I resisted, pressing my elbows into the desk.

I told myself to breathe—to use my breath to fan the flames of pain. Every cell of my body was on fire. Hunched over my desk, I wanted to hate him. I wanted to yell at him. I wanted to make it his fault that I was hurting. In a fit of determination, I switched off the lights and flung myself into bed, pulling my down comforter around me like a cocoon.

I was lost in a roaring furnace of rage. Caught in my own inferno, seeing myself caught, held in the fire, choosing the fire, wanting to die. I was dying. A part of me was dying.

Scenes flashed out of the fire. My brothers yelling "Witch hair! Girls not wanted," then a door closed locking me out. My father raged in my face as I shrank into the flames. I flipped from awareness to consumed, from consciousness to on fire. I had built my own pyre. I turned and twisted, wrestling with my comforter, every cell of my body hurting. I pleaded with myself, "I'm in my own worst nightmare of a black hole. Don't blame Don. It's not his fault." Then I was lost again—trembling, nauseous, sweating inside my cocoon. A small voice reminded me to breathe. It said, "Be the bellows of your own inferno. Burn away the pain." I breathed. The fire intensified and withered, flared, and receded. I lost myself in sleep, but the heat of my pyre awakened me to the reality of my dark cocoon again and again.

In between, I dreamt about Don. He was running through trees somewhere. I was running too, but he was too far ahead. I couldn't keep up. I was terrified. I couldn't run any faster. I couldn't see him any more. I was lost, scared, alone. I kept running, branches tearing at my clothes.

I jerked awake, lying in a pool of sweat, shivering. I faded in and out of consciousness for the rest of the night.

At about five in the morning, I was fully awake when some part of my awareness separated from the inferno. There was me and there was the inferno. There were two of us. I was confused. I saw myself from afar and yet up close. I experienced both in my mind— one light and free, one burning with rage. Then I was waiting, watching, no longer burning. Where did the inferno go? It seemed to be hovering over me, drifting slowly toward the window. I watched it go.

I was lost in limbo, white noise, feeling nothing. I waited, fully conscious, present and nowhere at the same time. Time seemed stuck. Then the top of my head began to tingle. It circled my head. Prickling marched over my face and crept down my neck. A sense of aliveness raced through my cells then, moving down my body. It flowed through my shoulders and arms, my breasts and back, my ribs and waist, like tiny sprinklers turning on in each cell, cleaning up ash from the inferno.

At seven in the morning, I began to move. I stretched. I wiggled my hips against the mattress and smoothed my hands over my body seeking something familiar. I felt the same, yet not the same. I had a sense of freedom, sparkling fresh and alive, like a morning glory in the cool dew of dawn.

I threw back my comforter, swung my long legs out of bed, planted my feet, and stretched for the ceiling. Awake from my fingers to my toes, I took a hot shower, which intensified the tingling. Every cell of my body felt alive and new born. I threw on clean jeans and a pullover. I couldn't wait to see Don.

As I got out of my car at the coffeehouse where we were meeting, he was walking across the parking lot toward me. I opened my arms. He pulled me into the warmth of his body. I molded to his form, swaying slightly. Anyone watching would have thought us lovers.

Without speaking, we got our drinks and settled into an old wooden table near the window. A hot tea warmed my hands. I congratulated him again. We talked about our work lives just as we always had. We decided to keep our coast property for now—the final piece of our divorce puzzle in place.

When we got up to leave, I offered Don a ride home. He accepted. In the car, I told him that I missed him and still cared about him. I had no expectations or hopes. Don said that he cared about me too, but I knew he was just being polite. Even that was all right with me. I stopped the car in front of his house, he got out, and said thanks. I watched as he trudged up the stone steps and disappeared into his new life. I felt like I had just read the last page and closed the cover on a great book—complete.

To release a black hole on my own, I had to feel my pain and also be aware of my body feeling pain. The key for me was to hold both realities in my energy field—my nightmarish black hole and the larger sense of who I am. When I was able to hold both, my awareness struggled to resolve the incongruity. Which one was the real me? On some level I chose, but I was not aware of the choice. My job was to hold two experiences in my conscious attention at the same time, so I could release my black hole. It took me all night to get there.

When you notice that a part of your body is tense, that you are feeling anxious, a little down, or frustrated, stop for a few minutes and sit quietly. You may be able to release a black hole on your own. Explore your reaction. Notice the sensation in your body. Breathe into it. You may be able to merge into greater comfort and learn something about yourself. If your reaction doesn't change, there may be more to discover when you have more time. Some black holes are such a fundamental way of life that they take some time to release. For these, have patience with yourself, and find a good friend or professional guide to talk with regularly. Other than taking more time, the process is the same—experience your black hole, explore your black hole's story or physical sensations, and accept and expand what you find.

Whether you find the release point through understanding in the mind-centered process or through physical sensations in the body-centered process, the essential ingredient is to allow yourself to feel vulnerable, scared, or hurt, and observe yourself experiencing these tender emotions. Allow your discomfort to expand and dissipate into an energy field of loving acceptance. The reward for embracing and releasing the experiences stored in your black holes is self-acceptance, freedom, and balanced energy.

All of what we believe, think, feel, hope, and experience is always with us. We don't get rid of anything. The black hole-releasing processes in this chapter gives us the freedom to accept and love ourselves as we are. Acceptance of who we've been balances our energy and allows us to become more of who we would like to be.

> *I still have all the neuroses I ever had. Only now they come to me like little schmoos and I greet them. Hello anger, hello lust, hello jealousy, hello envy. They no longer take over my personality and command my actions.*
>
> —RAM DASS

Chapter Six

Core Conversations and Core Information

....

I sat across the table from Nancy in an Italian restaurant in Portland. I was getting used to seeing her in her wig. She grinned at me from behind her menu when I told her how great she looked. "I'm glad they encouraged me to get this wig before my hair fell out," she said matter-of-factly. "I don't know what I would have done without the wig. I feel publicly presentable in it."

After we had ordered and the waiter left Nancy said, "I'm so hungry. I can't believe how much I eat now, but they reassured me that this is normal for someone on chemo." "Nancy, you seem so upbeat. How are you doing, really?"

"Part of the reason I wanted to have lunch with you today is that I've had some bad news." She lowered her eyes, giving herself time. "The last time I went in for chemo, I had a minor seizure, so they did a brain scan. The results were like ice water thrown in my face. They found 30 tumors in my brain. They're tiny now, but I have small-cell cancer. It's fast-growing and hard to fight, and chemo doesn't cross the blood-brain barrier. This significantly reduces my chances for survival. I'm scared, but I haven't given up. Tomorrow I start radiation treatments in addition to chemo." "Oh, Nancy." I slumped in my chair as tears stung my eyelids. "My heart aches when you say that. I'm amazed at how well you're taking this."

"I don't see that I have much choice. I'm doing everything that I can think of to beat this and I'm not giving up. I'm terrified and hopeful at the same time. I want all the ideas you have for what I can do to get well."

Nancy was scared. She understood what was happening to her and knew she wanted to live. This most recent crisis forced her to accept the reality of her situation and focus on her slim hope for survival. She wanted my help in exploring all the possibilities available to help her beat those odds. So though my chest ached for her, we were energized and connected at a core level. For the next couple of hours, we felt painfully alive as we created a plan for her to live.

In my conversation with Nancy, it would have been easy to say, "You'll get through this. You're going to be okay." But that would have hidden the sadness and concern I felt for her. It would have been easy for Nancy to tell me not to worry, but this in turn would have disguised her truth. Our reactions were painful, but honest.

When people share their honest feelings, thoughts, and wants with each other, they are engaged in core conversation. There is no pretense, no pirating, no hiding of core information. Core conversations cut to the essence of our desires, our perspectives, and our emotional reactions. Core conversations are clean and balanced; there is no agenda, no advice giving, no leading questions. Each participant is authentic and speaks only for himself.

You can decrease your energy flow by putting on a public face and denying your reactions, or you can allow your creative energy to flow freely. Human energy fields are balanced when energy flows freely—not constrained by energy pirating. Balanced energy is more available to consciously attract what you want in your life.

Core conversations can help you balance your energy and pour your creativity into what's important to you. You often have a choice about whether to reveal your honest reaction to someone, or cover up your reactions with polite conversation. When you hide your genuine reactions and talk about something else, you lose creative momentum. What you communicate, what you don't communicate, and how well you notice your own reactions can either allow your energy to flow toward balance, or it can reinforce pirate patterns and black holes.

Core conversations exchange core information, which is similar to formative information. In Chapter 1, I defined formative information as creative energy that calls into being that which matches or complements our emotions, beliefs, and intentions. Core information has the same three groups of information—feelings (emotions), thoughts (beliefs), and wants (intentions). However, core information is broader than formative information. For example, thought energy includes our beliefs and all our other thinking functions such as what we understand, our assumptions, the way we analyze a situation, our ideas. Beliefs are one of the forms of thought energy.

Specifically, core information includes the following:

Our Feelings—our emotions such as: anger, boredom, compassion, confusion, disappointment, excitement, fear, frustration, jealousy, joy, love, sadness, worry, and our physical sensations such as: feeling tense, hot, tired, nervous, uncomfortable, distress, pain.

Our Thoughts—our beliefs, thoughts, judgments, assumptions, stories, expectations, plans, philosophy—how we explain things to ourselves, how we understand or interpret what happens in our lives. This is our intellect, analysis, logic, and reasoning, which helps us understand our lives.

Our Wants—our wishes, desires, interests, hopes, and dreams. What we want in our lives. What we would like to have happen— our dreams of happiness, our intentions in each situation.

Feelings, thoughts, and wants are the elements we use in core conversations. In the very center is our core self, our soul, our spirit, the part of us that is eternal. Our core self goes beyond behavior, words, actions, beliefs, thoughts, feelings, and desires. Our core self is the observer of our thoughts, words, actions, and feelings. When we observe our reactions, we are not caught up in them. We are at peace with our humanness, and our energy expands with acceptance for others and ourselves.

At our core we are Capable, Open, Resourceful, and Empowered, the initial capital letters forming the acronym CORE. We feel capable of doing everything we want to do. We are open to our own core experience and to the feelings, thoughts, and wants of others. We feel resourceful and know that we can bring together money, people, places, and goods to accomplish our desires. Our potential seems empowered and unlimited. It is an experience of grace, gratitude, and expansive energy. We are who we really are—our energy fields at our best. We know that we are living the rare gift of human life and are capable of accepting and loving everyone at a core level, and most of all, ourselves. Few people stay permanently balanced in their core. Most of us flow in and out of our core experience.

When I share my core information with someone, I use the word "I" or "my." Some of us have been told that the word "I" seems selfish or boastful. However, since no one else has the same core experience that you have, when you share core information, the clearest word to use is "I" or "my." Many of us have been taught that it is better to say "we" instead of "I." And in two situations it is more appropriate: when we are in agreement and when we have accomplished something together.

Often, other people can sense your core energy—how you're feeling, what you're thinking, or what you want. If the core information (emotions, thoughts, wants) you communicate through your energy doesn't match your words, the person with whom you are interacting struggles to make sense of the inconsistency while you waste energy. The resulting interaction is out of balance. Your energy doesn't flow easily, and your ability to develop satisfying and creative outcomes from your conversations is truncated. For example, in the story at the beginning of the chapter, if Nancy had told me that she was fine, instead of seeking my help, we wouldn't have generated a plan. The plan didn't guarantee her survival, but we created more options for her than if we had both pretended everything would be fine.

When I am willing to share my core information with you, I am inviting you to join me in a core conversation. When you respond with your feelings, thoughts, and wants, we are engaging in conversation at the core of who we are. This conversation is not static. It flows with emotional energy. Emotions connect us. If you know what I'm feeling, you can understand my reactions and empathy builds a bridge—a bridge that connects us. If I understand your frustrations, my understanding increases our relationship. As our conversation deepens, a growing energy level sustains our relationship.

Do you remember a time when you had a different perspective from someone else on an issue, perhaps even a conflict, and you were really honest about it? Think back to a situation when you genuinely owned up to what you did or said? Did it lead to a deeper connection with the other person involved? If that person responded with the same level of honesty, the experience might have been a turning point in your relationship—a strengthening of your caring and connection. Unfortunately, core interactions are not common. When emotions flare, we tend to discount or give up on each other too easily.

I believe most people consider themselves honest and want sincere relationships, but I also believe that most people unconsciously hide their core information. In my experience, pirate patterns are more common than core conversations. When core information is missing in a relationship, the people involved do not feel entirely safe. They don't know where the triggers and black holes are. They don't know when a pirate pattern might emerge. This keeps conversations on the surface, as the people protect their core feelings, thoughts, and wants by keeping them hidden.

To risk being your real self in a world of energy pirating can be frightening. Like most of us, you probably feel safer behind your public face. But taking the risk of revealing the truth of your experience to others can help you dismantle your pirate patterns and invite others to do the same. If someone pirating energy doesn't get the reaction he is seeking, it throws off his strategy. Pirate strategies don't work as well when we speak honestly from our hearts.

Most people cover up their true feelings and intentions by being polite, needing to be right, or testing to see what will be acceptable to others. When I was head of the electric utility, I believed that being polite was more important than being honest. When a board member said something I disagreed with, I politely changed the subject. If he persisted, I volunteered to check with other board members about the issue. These were the subtle ways I hid my core information.

When we were growing up, we adapted to our environment in order to survive or succeed. We learned pirate patterns that were necessary for us to thrive or at least endure our early years. In the maturing process, there comes a time to grow beyond survival strategies and pirate patterns and reveal the authentic self. If we mature successfully, we learn to accept ourselves as we are. The concept of aligning ourselves with our core information is ancient wisdom, a part of human history. In order to be true to ourselves, we must have a balanced awareness of our core information.

Core conversations require discipline, practice, and the willingness to risk. Even after many years of teaching the art of core conversation, there are moments when I want to retreat behind face-saving niceties. And I do have that choice. How honest do I want to be? How safe am I with you? Can I risk really being who I am? Am I willing to live what I believe in every moment or just in safe, convenient moments? For me, creating core conversations by sharing my core information has fundamentally transformed how I interact with everyone in my life.

CLAIMING OUR CORE INFORMATION

Claiming our core information is easier said than done, and we may feel uncomfortable with what we find. If we prefer to be pleasant and cheerful, we may find feelings of frustration, anger, and disappointment. If we have become cynical, we may find deep caring and sadness. If money is important to us, we may find that what we really want is love. However, if we can allow ourselves to be simply curious and accept what we find, we will be rewarded with more balanced and focused creative energy.

Feelings

The first element of core information is our emotional responses and the physical sensations associated with them. This is our full range of feelings. Our joy and our excitement are tucked in next to our pain and our sorrow. Physical sensations, such as tightness, tension, and discomfort, help us find our emotions.

Emotions are powerful energy. Think of a time when you felt

excited or exuberant and your whole body felt energized. Think of a time when you were angry. Whether you held it back, leaked it out in sarcastic comments, or exploded in rage, the emotional energy of your anger was intense. People speak of venting anger. However, it's energy that is vented—energy that flows from emotion. The grieving process—experiencing sorrow, anger, sadness, pain, and loss—is enormously draining, but hiding your emotions in black holes where the energy is trapped is even more tiring because it stretches over a much longer period of time. Releasing emotions may reduce your energy for a few hours; withholding feelings can depress your energy for years. In Holland, an enormous amount of energy is spent on building and maintaining a system of dikes to hold back the sea. Similarly, we expend enormous energy trying to hold back the tide of our emotions so that we don't feel them.

Some people give themselves the freedom to experience their emotions moment to moment, allowing the tide to flow. They are acutely aware of their sensations and emotions and choose to use them as guides for decisions and choices in life. I am still learning to allow myself to fully experience my emotions. Every morning when I read the newspaper, I am drawn to the sweet, sad, human-interest stories because they touch my heart. Often I have tears in my eyes as I read them. Rather than avoiding this sorrow, I appreciate feeling it because it reminds me that I am fully alive.

I don't think our culture shares my interest in emotional freedom. By freedom, I don't mean the license to act out my emotions, but the freedom to internally experience my feelings. I believe that Western culture doesn't encourage or support the release and flow of natural emotions. But we do need emotional information for guidance. Our emotions are similar to instincts. Animals instinctually know when to migrate. These are not logical, rational decisions. Geese do not count the days or look at the temperature before flying south. They have a feel for the right time and direction. We may have diminished our natural instincts by burying our emotions. Similar to instinct in animals, we may find core emotional information valuable for making better choices for living.

When we feel tense, afraid to walk down a dark street, our body is warning us of danger. Fear is useful information meant to protect us. Fear can also be irrational and unfounded, however. When fear has been hidden in black holes, we may feel terrified when there is little actual current danger. As we learn to accept our emotions and separate the valuable information from automatic behavior (like stomping in rage, withdrawing in frustration) and black hole reactions, emotional information can guide us and help us make more informed life choices.

Thoughts

Our thinking is usually, but not always the easiest of the three elements of core experience to access. This is the cognitive, analytical part of us. School systems help students develop their intellectual thinking abilities. Our interpretations, beliefs, logic, thoughts, assumptions, and reasoning lead us to an understanding of the world around us. This part of our awareness interprets events and situations. It includes our stories, our beliefs, and our assumptions about the world. Our stories are what we tell ourselves about what has happened in our lives. Our stories are not necessarily what really happened, but are interpretations of what happened. Our assumptions and beliefs arise from our stories. And, as we learn more about ourselves, we can change our stories, and consequently our beliefs and assumptions.

Stories with intense emotional consequences sometimes become secrets. No one wants to deal with the emotional consequences of revealing a secret, so it remains untold. Families sometimes hold on to secrets for generations. Some common family secrets include child and spousal abuse, alcoholism, mental illness, prison time, and death. Secrets are shared black holes. Family energy is consumed in keeping these secrets. When the secrets are told, acknowledged, and accepted—when the truth is spoken—energy is released.

Stories are not purely intellectual memory. Stories are emotional memories. When we fully remember something that has occurred in our lives, we can feel the emotions and sensations linked to that experience. We cannot even separate purely scientific information from our emotions. Scientists often react to their findings with satisfaction or with frustration, sometimes feeling competitive or passionate about their work. We are emotional beings. Our thinking process is chemically linked to our emotions and physical sensations.

Since emotions influence human energy, tapping into our history and our stories releases energy that has been held in our emotional memories. As human beings, our thinking triggers emotions and physical sensations, which in turn engage our intellectual and analytical processes to understand what we are feeling. Since emotional energy is linked to thinking, emotional energy is influenced by how we perceive our life situations. For example, if we think we are in danger, fear energy in the form of adrenaline boosts our energy. If we think we have wasted our life, we may feel depressed, which reduces our energy. Our thoughts and perceptions directly affect our emotional energy. Therefore, though few of us do this easily, it is possible to shift our energy with our thoughts. This is what happens when we release black holes.

Intentions

The third part of our core information guides our future; it includes our wants, intentions, interests, wishes, desires, hopes, and dreams. It is nearly impossible to create what we want in life unless we consciously or unconsciously know what it is.

Our wants, desires, interests, and intentions guide us through life. What kind of work do we want to do? Whom do we want to spend time with? Do we want to have children? Where do we want to go on vacation? What do we want for dinner? What do we want to do tonight? What do we want for our community, our country, the world?

For most of us, knowing and acting on our basic wants is easy. For example: "I'm hungry, let's eat." "I'd like a ride to school." "The neighbors invited us over. I'd like to go." Author and psychologist, Abraham H. Maslow, defined a hierarchy of needs that govern our intentions: survival, safety, acceptance, self-esteem, self-actualization. Until our basic needs are met, other interests higher on Maslow's scale will not be as important. Air, water, and food are the most essential needs. Then shelter becomes a priority. Safety is more important to us than being part of a group. Then we need acceptance and recognition before we develop self-esteem and self-actualization.

Needs are also wants. Usually, needs have a condition attached to them. For example, I need to breathe and eat if I want to live. The need is a condition of what I want, which is to live. The phrase, "I need your help," implies desperation. The phrase, "I want your help," more accurately acknowledges the other person's freedom to help or not. In interactions, I try to convert my "needs" to "wants," and if I can't let go of my desperation, I try to state that outright. For example, I might say, "I really want your help and I'm feeling desperate." This more accurately reflects the truth of the situation while respecting the other person's right to choose. Fine-tuning my words to more accurately reflect my core information maintains more balance in my energy field.

Our emotional memories, beliefs, and assumptions all influence our interests and desires. If we have difficulty identifying our interests and what we want, we may have emotional memories stored in black holes. Black holes hide information from us. Without exploring and understanding our stories, beliefs, and assumptions, we may not know what we want. For example, if you stuffed the abuse you suffered as a child into a black hole, you may deny your longing for all children to be safe. If you blocked your childhood passion for rivers, you may not realize your desire to protect watersheds. If you put away your natural childhood curiosity and wonder, you may not find your passion for exploring or teaching or coaching others. True, long-term interests are influenced by our emotional memories. Emotional memories provide essential information for us to make healthy choices. People who can't access healthy emotional information have a hard time finding their life purpose and passion. Satisfying apparent desires, without access to emotional memories, can result in devastating consequences. Such are the choices of addicts and people in prison.

For example, Barry unconsciously felt he was a burden to his family. When he was a child, his family struggled financially and

Barry decided they would be better off if he hadn't been born. He hid this story in a black hole and covered up his feelings with alcohol. After Barry kicked his addiction and faced his life story, he discovered his passion for working with teens to help them find productive places in their families and communities.

Getting what we truly want is energizing. Not getting what we want can reduce our energy. Think of a time when you achieved what you really wanted—a new job, a new car. Do you remember a rush of energy the moment you realized your dream was coming true? On the other hand, do you remember being disappointed or devastated by falling short of your goals or losing something you cared about like a pet? You may have had low energy for a few days or weeks, depending on how important it was to you.

True intentions and desires flow with life energy. How energized you feel can help you determine what you want. If a friend invites you to a party and you feel excited, you probably want to go. If the same invitation leaves you tired, you probably don't want to go. This simple example is clear. Apply this energy awareness to your job and career choices and notice what you find.

As we engage in core conversations, awareness of our energy expands to help us find what we truly want. Energy can help us discover and satisfy our wants and therefore expand our energy. Our wants are intimately linked with our life force energy.

FINDING OUR CORE INFORMATION

Awareness of our core information—our feelings, thoughts, and wants—comes from the small voice inside us that speaks in our heads and our hearts. I use the following questions to find the three elements of my core information. I ask each question, then stop and listen to my quiet inner voice. Try these: How am I feeling right now? What's that about? What do I want right now?

The first question asks you to check in with your emotions and sensations in this moment. The best answer to this question is a one or two-word answer. For example, at this moment I'm sitting at my computer writing as the sun sets over the Pacific Ocean. If I were to answer the first question right now, I'd say I'm feeling peaceful.

Earlier today, as I sat on my deck in the rare Oregon sunshine, my answer would have been "grateful." Sometimes when I'm writing, I feel frustrated or stuck.

If our heads are filled with confusing thoughts or strong warnings, we may be hearing the voice of fear. If so, then the answer might be, "I'm afraid to say how I'm feeling" or "I'm feeling confused or numb." Emotions are often layered—that is, one emotion covers up or hides another deeper emotion. Confusion may cover anger. Anger may hide fear. Feeling numb can mask terror. Frustration may cover up hopelessness. Cynicism may disguise caring. As we embrace each layer of emotional information, it gives way to the next, like layers of an onion. Our small voice shows up more clearly as we accept and acknowledge the deeper layers of our emotions. As you read this paragraph, how are you feeling right now? What one or two words best describe your emotions? Blank? Curious? Confused? Sleepy? Sad? Excited?

When I first began to develop my awareness of in-the-moment core information, I didn't have a clear sense of how I was feeling unless I was angry. And then there was someone to blame. I didn't realize that my anger arose from me. I used to think that other people caused me to be angry. Now I know that my emotions are mine—perhaps triggered by other people and events, but the triggers are mine, too.

Emotions signal where we are coming from—why we are involved, why we say what we say and do what we do. Our emotions motivate us. We move toward what gives us pleasure and away from what gives us pain. We are motivated by how we think we will feel in a given situation based on past experiences. The following shows how adding emotional information to a statement adds meaning.

"The report is due on Tuesday. I want to get started." This statement doesn't reveal what is motivating the speaker.

By adding emotion, the motivation becomes clearer: "I'm relieved that the report is due on Tuesday. I want to get started." Notice how more of the person is revealed.

Alternatively, a different emotion changes the picture: "I'm afraid that the report is due on Tuesday. I want to get started."

People generally have dissimilar emotions in similar situations. Their emotions likely will be governed by the presence or absence of triggers and black holes. For example, think of the reactions people have when you are late. Some people don't notice. Some don't care. Some are worried about you. Some are irritated when you weren't on time. Did you cause each of their reactions by being late, or do their reactions belong to them?

Once I realized that my emotions are mine, I wanted to find out what I was feeling. Most of the time, I wasn't aware of feeling anything. So, I started with two emotions that I could accept and discern easily—feeling comfortable and feeling uncomfortable. Ask yourself: Am I comfortable or uncomfortable right now? Start with these two and expand your awareness to other feelings.

Emotions provide a powerful means of connection among family, friends, and co-workers. If a friend is brokenhearted, a family member is upset, a co-worker is frustrated, these feelings, if revealed, connect us with that person's experience. When we know how someone feels, we can have compassion and empathy for him. Without emotion, there is little room for human understanding and connection. Shared emotions create human connection. Relationship energy is born of human connection. Relationship energy is like electricity, which flows when the breakers are in contact. We use the word "touched"—as in "I feel touched by your story"—to express a connection.

The second question to ask yourself in the process of becoming aware of your core information—what's that about?—taps our thinking and provides context for our emotions and intentions. This question engages our analytical thinking. We may review past experiences to understand what we are feeling. What brings up this feeling? Is something that just happened similar to a past experience? Are the feelings similar? This question can bring up our stories. Emotions we are experiencing in this current moment may actually be from the past. By describing what has happened in the past, we can understand and accept our current feelings more easily, and become aware of what we truly want.

How are you feeling right now and what's that about? If you are feeling uncomfortable or confused, you may have triggered a black hole. If so, the answer to the question "What's that about?" is "I've triggered a black hole." That may be all I'm aware of at first. Later I may be able to identify feeling embarrassed and inadequate because I've made a mistake, or say more about the black hole that has been triggered.

The third question—what do I want right now?— is dependent on the other two questions. It is the movement toward thoughtful action. Yet many people have lost touch with their true intentions. How many times have you asked someone what she wants and her response is "I don't know" or "I don't care." Without clear emotional guides and an understanding of what is going on, it's hard to know what results you want to create. The first two questions, getting at feelings and thoughts, lead the way to wants. If you are feeling uncomfortable or confused and you have triggered a black hole, the answer to the question "What do I want right now?" may be, "I want to know more about how to release black holes" or "I want to feel comfortable again."

When you choose an action without connecting your thoughts and feelings to it, you may later regret your choice. These three simple questions can help you understand and accept your core information.

Many people have trouble finding their core information, and may instead feel foggy or confused when they ask themselves these three questions. Sometimes this information is completely inaccessible—loaded in a black hole and put away. Pirate patterns keep disturbing emotions and beliefs stored in black holes from surfacing. When core information is partially inaccessible, some people prefer to rely on analysis, logic, and reasoning. Others act solely on feelings without thinking things through. Some act without thinking or feeling, while others simply put off action. It is easier to make important life decisions and the choices we make will be more in line with who we truly are when we acknowledge and accept our core information.

If you find yourself relying primarily on one or two of the

elements of core information, your energy is out of balance. One group of information may dominate and exclude important information from another group. For example, if you prefer to solve problems with reasoning and analysis, you may be missing critical emotional information. This information may be hidden in a black hole. On the other hand, if you tend to solve problems primarily by venting and feeling your way along, you may be missing critical thinking information. I have encountered few people in the corporate world who solve problems with a full complement of core information.

If you notice a void of emotional information, simply ask yourself how you are feeling. Accept your sensations as clues to your emotions. Tension or anxiety may suggest fear. Loss of energy may be sadness or grieving. Twitching can be irritation or anger. Flushing or turning red may be humiliation, embarrassment, or shame. By accessing your emotional core information, you will be able to balance your energy and create a better solution.

If you get lost in your emotions, ask yourself what they are about. Notice what triggered them. Tell yourself the story of what is going on. Talk with others to help you understand the situation that is triggering your feelings. Identify specifically which elements of your situation trigger your most intense reactions. Gather more information about the situation to balance your emotional energy with understanding.

If you don't have clear wants, ask yourself questions. What do I want? What do I want to do about my situation? If you are reading and notice that you are feeling sad, ask yourself what that's about. Once you identify the specific passage that triggered your reaction, and how it relates to your life, ask yourself the question "What do I want?" Given your reaction and the specific reference that triggered it, what would you like to have happen and what do you what to do about it? For example, if your reaction to my mom's or Nancy's story is sadness, perhaps there is someone in your life with cancer and you want to contact her and have a core conversation. Perhaps you have lost someone to cancer and want to allow yourself time to grieve.

Give yourself time to allow your interests to emerge from your understanding and emotions. By gathering all the elements of essential information, you balance your energy; your connections with others will be deeper, you will be able to have core conversations, and the actions that emerge from your wants will be more creative and satisfying.

You can have core conversations any time and anywhere. The following example contrasts an interaction characterized by pirate patterns with a core conversation. There is nothing remarkable about the first interaction. It is a normal disagreement, the kind that occurs at many workplaces. Many of us have participated in such an exchange. The interaction is then repeated to show how the outcome can change when the players share their core information.

———————— • • • • • ————————

A Conversation Illustrating Pirate Patterns

Cliff and Bill work for a management consulting firm. They were meeting to design a leadership training program for a large corporate client. "Why can't he see what I'm talking about?" Cliff thought to himself. He told Bill, "You're not listening to me. I've got a solution to this design problem, but we're not getting anywhere." Bill replied, "Cliff, I've been listening to you for an hour. We've used up half our time going nowhere. The boss is going to be all over me if I don't have a solution by noon. I don't see how your idea can work. Give it up." Bill tossed his pen on the papers in front of him.

Cliff clenched his jaw and thought, "If he doesn't want to hear my idea, let him try to find something better. His butt is on the line. I'm sure as hell not going to help. What do I care?" But all he said was, "Fine. What are you going to report to the boss?" Bill replied, "I'm going to report the plan we've always used, unless we come up with something better."

Cliff commented, "I thought the boss wanted something new." Bill answered, "Well, he does. So we've got to come up with some changes to this program to make it look new. What other ideas do you have?"

Folding his arms across his chest, Cliff responded, "I don't have any ideas."

Cliff gave up trying to explain his idea to Bill. Cliff was using the distant/indifferent pirate pattern. Bill lost the benefit of Cliff's energy, ideas, and commitment to the project. Bill was irritated with Cliff for not contributing. Bill was using the intimidator/self-righteous pirate pattern. He felt frustrated and drained. Cliff felt de-energized.

———— • • • • • ————

Have you seen interactions like this at your workplace? Do you recognize similar conversations with your spouse or your family? Perhaps your children respond as Cliff did. Teenagers regularly disengage from their parents. In your experience, do disagreements surface or do conflicts go underground?

A Core Conversation

"Why can't Bill see what I'm talking about?" Cliff thought to himself. He said aloud, "I'm really struggling with this conversation. I can't seem to describe my idea in a way that makes sense. I really want you to understand it. Then if you don't like it, that's okay with me, but right now I'm frustrated." "I'm frustrated too," Bill replied. "We've been at this program design for almost an hour and I can't see that we've made any progress. I've got to be in the boss's office at noon with a new version of this training program and I'm afraid I won't have anything to report."

Cliff answered, "It's 11 o'clock now, so that gives us another hour. I really believe that I've got the solution to this design problem. If I could just say it right, I think our work would be done. I need about ten minutes to describe it. That leaves us fifty minutes to come up with something else if you don't like it. Otherwise, I'm afraid I'll be stuck feeling frustrated and not very helpful." Bill was interested. "If my undivided attention for ten minutes will get us through this impasse, I'll really try to listen to your idea. If I understand it and like it, great. If I understand it and don't like it, will you help me come up with something else?"

Cliff agreed, "Yes, if you really understand it and you don't like it, then I'll drop it and help you develop something else." Bill clinched the agreement, "Okay. Go for it."

These two business associates still aren't agreeing on their design, but each one is willing to speak his core information and listen to the other. When Cliff began his description, he was fully invested in the idea, but also willing to let go of it.

Bill was fully engaged in trying to understand Cliff's perspective as the best way to get what he wanted—a report for the boss by noon. This core conversation opened the door for both players to get what they wanted. Each was honest about his frustrations and committed to finding a solution that would work for both of them. The result was an energized discussion that led to a collaborative solution and a positive outcome for the client. This core conversation energized both Cliff and Bill.

——————— • • • • • ———————

That's all well and good, you say, but what if I'm the only one committed to having a core conversation? What if I share my core information and the other person continues pirating? What if I am the only one willing to be honest? Here is another interaction.

——————— • • • • • ———————

Karen hesitantly joined the line at the counter. She hated returning merchandise, and the saleswoman seemed to be in a hurry and hadn't been very helpful with the last customer. When it was Karen's turn, she stepped forward and began, "This leather coat doesn't fit me. Your tailor was going to let down the sleeves. You said it would be long enough for me, but it isn't." "Look," said the clerk. "We can't take back a coat once it has been altered. It's yours."

"Well, I can't wear it like this, and I don't want it," said Karen, her pulse quickening and her face turning red. The clerk repeated, "You had it altered. I can't do anything about it."

"Well, I'm not taking it with me. I'm leaving it here and I'm getting my money back, even if I have to take you to court." Karen threw the coat on the counter and marched out of the store, feeling indignant.

Karen blamed the tailor for not fixing her leather jacket. She believed the store was at fault and was angry at the clerk. Karen threw some of her emotional energy on the counter along with her jacket and left the store. She probably replayed the scene a number of times in her mind on the way home, venting even more energy. Karen could spend the next few months dealing with small claims court before getting her money back, and she would still not have the leather coat she wanted. Is there another way to conduct this conversation? What will happen if Karen claims her core information—her honest unhappy feelings? Will it make a difference if she talks about what happened and asks specifically for what she wants? The same clerk is in the following scenario. Notice the change in both Karen and the clerk.

——————— · · · · · ———————

When it was Karen's turn, she stepped forward, "I'm feeling nervous about returning this coat, and you seem in a hurry. Is there someone I can talk to about my problem?" "I'm the only one here. The manager will be back in half an hour. You can wait if you want to."

"I'd prefer to talk with you, if you have the time. Then, if we don't come up with a solution, I'll wait for the manager. Would that work for you?" "As long as I don't have any other customers, go ahead. What's the problem?"

"I'm feeling really frustrated about this coat because I had it altered, but the sleeves still aren't long enough and I'm not comfortable wearing it. Is there anything we can do to get a coat that fits me?" "Did our tailor alter it?"

"Yes." "Okay. Put it on, let me see how it fits."

Karen slipped into the coat. The clerk studied her sleeve length and shook her head. "It's almost the right length, but it's a little short. Let me check with the tailor and see if there's anything that he can do. If not, I'll check with the manager and see what she can do. I gotta tell you, the store policy is no returns for altered merchandise, and no returns for cash, credit only. But maybe there's something we can do. Can you wait a week?" "I'd love to have it sooner, but I want a coat that fits. So take the time you need to make it fit right."

The clerk thought, "She seems like a nice person. Maybe there is something I can do." Karen took the coat off and handed it to the clerk, relaxing for the first time since she came into the store. "Thank you so much for your help. I was worried about how this would turn out. You've been very helpful."

In the first interaction, Karen fueled her anger by deflating the clerk with accusations. She hid her truth, which was that she was frustrated. She protected herself from recognizing this discomfort by blaming the store.

In the second interaction, Karen acknowledged the clerk's situation. She invited the clerk's participation by letting her know what was going on for her emotionally. She was clear about what she wanted. Finally, Karen acknowledged the clerk's contribution. Karen explored the truth of her experience and invited the clerk into a core conversation.

─────── • • • • • ───────

Connecting emotionally with others and moving toward what we each want is engaging and energizing. Core conversations release group energy the way exploring black holes releases personal energy. Released energy flows into creative solutions. Core conversation is simple and clean. It doesn't plug the flow of energy with black holes and pirate patterns. Personal energy is not bound up in blame, denial, protection, excuses, or pirate strategies. These energy traps are set aside. When we are centered in our core truth, aligned with our integrity, trusting and accepting ourselves, and clear about our wants, we are filled with energy. This energy cannot be taken from us unless we choose to give it away. In fact, if two of us are sharing core information with integrity and acceptance, creative, expansive, balanced energy fills our energy fields and affects others. We need not be in a happy frame of mind for this energy to be created. In fact, many times we are sad, troubled, concerned, uncertain, or frustrated. Yet, even with these emotions, there is power and energy in acknowledging and speaking from our core.

Core conversations are different from traditional creative

problem solving, conflict resolution, or assertiveness training. These other approaches add techniques to our repertoire of skills and abilities. We can continue our pirate patterns and still learn problem solving and assertiveness techniques. These tools may even assist us in more effective pirating.

Core conversations are the opposite of learning techniques. Saying our core truth means setting aside our protective (pirating) patterns—our masks—and exploring our genuine emotions, true desires, and deeply held beliefs. Core conversations help us understand our motivations, and explore and discover the authentic us—who are we at our core, including our vulnerabilities and our strengths. If you haven't explored in this way before, you may feel anxious or reluctant at first.

FROM BLACK HOLES AND PIRATE PATTERNS TO CORE CONVERSATIONS

Black holes encourage us to see others as the cause of whatever difficulties we are experiencing and think they need to change so we can feel better. We avoid and protect our black holes by pirating energy. In a core conversation, we take ownership of our core experience, and recognize that we can influence the course of our lives. No one else will respond to the situation in exactly the same way as we do because our reactions are based on our life experiences.

If you find yourself in a pirate pattern, acknowledge yourself for recognizing it. Ask yourself the three questions that will help you find your core self: How am I feeling right now, what's that about, and what do I want? Exploring your pirate patterns and black holes will help you learn how to have core conversations. The intensity of your reactions can help you identify your core emotions and explore what triggers them. Disclosing your feelings, saying what's going on for you, and asking for what you want is the best way to change your patterns. None of us like claiming our pirate patterns, but owning them is the first and most important step in not engaging in them. The following example shows how to shift from a black hole reaction to a core conversation.

I found myself in an angry, blaming, righteous pirate pattern with my son. Travis was a junior at the University of Oregon. Three weeks before fall term ended, he came home and announced that he was dropping out of school—too late in the term to get our tuition back. Since I was helping to pay for his education, I had a black hole reaction. My reaction, which thankfully I didn't voice, was, "You can't drop out. We've paid too much money. You must not be working hard enough, so get to work and finish this term." That was my self-righteous pirate pattern. I let that thought go and asked myself how I was feeling and what I wanted. Then I responded to Travis' announcement. "I'm frustrated, Travis. I wonder if you're working hard enough, and I'd like you to stay in school after all the money we've spent." "I thought you'd feel that way," he said. "But I just don't know what I'm doing in school right now and I need some time to sort this out."

I thought for a moment and looked for the next layer of my core information. "What's really going on is that I'm feeling scared. I'm afraid that if you drop out you won't finish school, and I believe that a good education is essential for everything you want." "I know that, Mom, but I'm really confused right now. I don't know what I want to do with my life. I'd like to spend the winter skiing and thinking about things. I'm not going back."

"You know, Trav, what's behind the fear is so much love. I love you so very much. I really believe that you are smart and capable, and I want you to finish your degree. I think it will open up opportunities for you that will make your life more enjoyable."

I had moved myself from self-righteous pirating to my core information in just a few minutes by asking myself the core questions. As for Travis, he spent the winter in a cabin at a ski resort, managing a small restaurant and ski rental business. He read more books that winter than he had in any of his college semesters. In the spring, when he was ready to return to school, I was thrilled.

Our core conversation kept the energy balanced in our relationship. We stayed connected and open to each other's lives.

Later, when he finished his degree, he moved to Alaska to kayak and ski. All I can do is support and love my son; the rest is up to him. Core conversations allow me to do that.

Once we've opened to our core and shared information, we may feel vulnerable. We may notice our human frailties, and experience frustration, fear, and a sense of loss. We may need practice talking about our core experiences. The following are examples of core statements:

- I'm angry and I feel like lashing out, but I don't really want to.
- I'm really frustrated that I haven't been able to get across some information that's important to me. I'd like to take another shot at it.
- I'm uncomfortable with the direction we're taking. I think there's a solution we haven't thought of yet, and I'd like to hear from each person in the group before we proceed.
- I'm in a black hole right now and I need a little time to explore what's going on for me. Can we continue this conversation when I feel more balanced?
- I'm feeling vulnerable and scared, and I'd like your help while I sort through what's going on for me.

When we first begin to share core information honestly, it may feel risky. We are taking a chance that the other person won't pirate more energy while we explore our core experience. We may need time to uncover deeper layers of our core experiences. I believe in second and third chances to try again with the same person to touch him with our core information. With each new response from someone, we have a new moment and a new core experience. When we are in the flow of expansive energy, our core experience changes moment to moment. An additional reaction from someone may trigger a new response in me. Each of my reactions is connected to a new understanding and perhaps even a new want. Here are the same examples of core statements followed by pirating answers. These examples show how to respond with a new core experience to each additional reaction. These interactions also show how it is possible to be our genuine core self in the face of pirating.

You say: "I'm angry and I feel like lashing out, but I don't really want to." The other person responds: "Oh, great, you get angry and lash out. Then I get angry. That's our pattern. Here we go again."

You have a new moment: "That has been our pattern in the past and I'm working on it. Although it's not easy for me to change, I'd like your help." If the other person continues pirating, he says: "You've been working on it for years and I haven't seen any change."

Your core response may be: "I'm feeling badly about how we're interacting right now. I'm going to take a break, but I'd like to talk later."

Your response has created the potential for a shift when you talk again.

You say: "I'm really frustrated that I haven't been able to get across some information that's important to me. I'd like to take another shot at it." The other person responds: "We've been listening to you all morning and you haven't said anything new yet. When are we going to get on with this meeting?"

You can say: "I have been taking up some time this morning, and I wish I'd been more clear from the beginning, but my perspective has been evolving as we've talked and now I'd like to summarize what I've learned."

You say: "I'm uncomfortable with the direction we're taking. I think there's a solution we haven't thought of yet, and I'd like to hear from each person in the group before we proceed." The other person responds: "We don't have time for this."

You can say: "I realize the time is short. I'm just afraid we're moving in the wrong direction. I'd feel a lot more comfortable if I hear what everyone thinks now, before we find ourselves down the road changing direction again."

You say: "I'm in a black hole right now, and I need a little time to explore what's going on for me. Can we continue this conversation later?" The other person responds: "Black hole! What the hell is a black hole?"

Your truth in the next moment might be: "I use the term 'black hole' when I'm feeling scared, frustrated, or uncomfortable. Right now I'm uncomfortable and I'd like some space to sort out my thoughts."

You say: "I'm feeling vulnerable and scared, and I'd like your help while I sort through what's going on for me." The other person responds: "I'm as gentle as a lamb." In truth, you may pause. You may even laugh. Then take his comment at face value: "I'm glad to hear that. I've not always seen you as a lamb. I could really appreciate that side of you right now."

Engaging in core conversation means sticking with yourself, trusting your feelings, and asking for what you want while staying connected and open to others. How many times should you continue to ask for what you want? The best guideline I've found is to ask myself, "How important is it?" If it's not very important, let it go. If it's very important, stick to it. In choosing how many times to ask for what you want, the key is to be open to others, listen, and be willing to be changed by what you hear. Relentlessly asking for what you want without listening can be righteous pirating. Understanding the other person's core experience can give you time to adjust your perspective and interests.

Once I faced a situation that was so important to me that I asked my spouse over fifty times for a talk to work things out. The first forty times, I had my black holes covered with several pirate strategies. The responses I got reflected my approach. The last ten times I began to share my core experience and to invite my spouse into a core conversation. The following conversation took place after I realized that I had to change in order to change the situation

I stood at the front door of the home I had moved out of several months before. I raised my hand to knock again, and wondered if Alan, my ex, would answer the door. Neighborhood kids were riding their tricycles on the sidewalk, calling to each other. A pang of regret stabbed me as I turned to watch them ride past. I wondered where my children were. I missed them when they were at Alan's.

The door opened and I was face to face with Alan. "What do you want?" He glared at me. I refused to get angry. "I'm feeling pretty nervous about talking with you. I know this is really tough for both of us. I'd like us to talk about what's best for our kids. Do you think you could talk with me today?"

"No, I've had it trying to talk to you about anything. You can talk to my lawyer." I refused the bait. "I'd really like to talk with you," I continued. "I think the best thing we can do for our kids is to share custody. The courts won't recognize joint custody unless we agree on how to share responsibility for our kids. I love them so very much and I know you do too. I'm willing to keep asking until you're ready to talk."

"I'm not ready to talk now," he said, closing the door. I stood for a moment, staring at the door. I thought, "As hard as this is, he didn't slam the door. I'll come back tomorrow."

I had made a commitment to my children and myself that they would have both parents involved and responsible for parenting. I had resolved to ask for what I wanted, joint custody, for as long as there was hope. Alan was hurt and angry, and fighting for sole custody. I had to build safety and trust so that he would talk with me. Once I was willing to be vulnerable and ask for what I wanted without insisting, or pushing, or making him "wrong," he did talk to me, and we worked out an agreement. The courts approved our joint-custody settlement in February of 1978. I moved to a house three blocks from Alan's and our kids grew up with the active involvement of both of us. I had stumbled into core conversation and discovered my core feelings, thoughts, and wants from this experience, because it was the only way there was enough safety and openness for Alan to be willing to talk with me. I discovered it after trying every pirate strategy I knew and finding that none of them worked.

EXPRESSING YOUR CORE EXPERIENCE

I have shared information about core conversations with hundreds of groups. Each time I ask whether feelings, thoughts, or wants were easiest to access. Only 5 percent of the people indicated that they consistently and clearly know what they want. Of the remaining 95 percent, about half indicate that they are most aware of their thinking and the other half are most aware of their feelings. When I work with business groups, however, many of them tell me they are reluctant to share their emotional awareness with co-workers.

When we are in a tough spot, we may try to shut off our emotions. We may feel scared, lost, hurt, or devastated. We may experience a black hole and feel out of control. We may be afraid to move through our day without falling apart. In a black hole, we may feel at the mercy of our emotions. Even when we feel overwhelmed, however, our emotions and intentions can be our guides.

Most people prefer to function with one or two core elements. Some people have spent their entire lives hiding their emotions or their wants, choosing instead to be ruled by their intellect. I think some people are afraid of their wants, because they judge their desires as unacceptable. Others don't want to be disappointed if they don't get what they want. These people protect themselves from their core experience. Some are troubled that they don't know what they are passionate about, not realizing that they are protecting themselves from knowing.

I think some people are afraid of their emotions because they have little practice allowing themselves to experience emotions. They act compulsively, instead of allowing their feelings to wash over them. When we are lost in our emotions, our feelings seem out of control, bigger than we are, and we feel compelled to react and behave automatically.

Many of us are beginning observers of our emotional selves. We have momentary experiences of wonder about our emotional reactions. As we mature, we learn to look at ourselves in the same way we might observe a beloved child—with curiosity and love. Releasing our black holes helps us practice emotional detachment, awareness, and acceptance. Every emotion has a purpose. None is banished from our core experience. All are acceptable. When we feel defensive and want to protect ourselves, we can say what's true for us. We can say, "I'm feeling defensive right now. I'd like a little time to understand what that's about."

Learning to accept and observe our emotions without acting allows us to open to a full range of emotions. A satisfying life is filled with emotion—the rapture of being in a sunlit wildflower meadow, the joy of seeing the twinkle in your daughter's eye, the feelings you have for a beloved family pet, the excitement of winning a race, the pleasure of seeing an old friend, the pride of a job well done. These experiences can be lost if we restrict our emotional awareness.

I would like us to take our feelings out of the closet and develop emotional information the way we have developed analytical thinking in the West. The scientific method of inquiry, our legal system, computer systems, and the Internet have all advanced human thinking. Now we are beginning to recognize that we are greatly influenced by our emotions. I have hope that we will develop healthy core emotional information the way we have developed healthy scientific thinking.

The importance of feelings is recognized by talk shows. Unfortunately, most talk radio and television shows sensationalize emotions and pirate patterns. Many shows encourage people to blame each other for their situation in life. These shows are popular, because black holes and pirate patterns create wonderful drama. Core emotions are less dramatic. They are tempered with detachment, acceptance, and understanding. Core conversations begin with listening to the small voice within you, acknowledging your core information, and being willing to talk about your core experiences.

There is a fine line between recognizing core information and running pirate patterns. Pirate patterns may seem normal while core information is hidden just below the surface. Other people's reactions to you can be helpful in determining the difference. If other people open up to what you are saying and respond with core information, you are probably balanced in your core experience. If other people become defensive, argumentative, or withdrawn, they may be reacting to a black hole trigger, or you may be pirating energy.

Our core truth is a gentle loving truth, not a harsh or brutal truth. It is simply accepting what's true for us—our core reactions, understandings, and desires. When our core information emerges into our consciousness, we may feel vulnerable. We may want to hold our core information like a newborn baby, gently, and with a sense of wonder. When we are ready to speak from our core, what we say shines like a flashlight in the darkness, illuminating our honest experience. When others stand close to us, they too are illuminated and experience energy from that light. When we accept our own core, people are attracted to us. People sense the light of truth and are drawn to it. Acceptance is like an oasis in a blame-filled world. When we are centered in the acceptance of our own core, we invite core information from others.

As each person speaks core information, understanding grows into agreement. Once there is understanding and agreement, we use the word "we" to indicate a shift from individual perspective to agreement. "We" is an especially wonderful word to use when we have worked and created something together.

The drivers of our lives are our core experiences. Our behaviors, actions, and what we say are formed on the foundation of our thoughts, feelings, and wants. Our core information gives our life meaning and direction. Core feelings, thoughts, and wants offer a road map for our well-being. At the very least, they influence us and allow us to influence those around us, because they are the motivators for our choices and actions in life. Yet many people hide this essential information. Core information is less reliable when we protect and disguise it. Perhaps as we grow toward an emotionally healthy culture, these core messages will be embraced and supported as essential for healthy lives.

If we want to be the architect of our own experience, be a good influence on those around us, and lead a full, high-energy life, we must become familiar with our core feelings, thoughts, and wants. Our willingness to share our core information is an invitation to others to do the same. Core conversations open doors of human connection that allow us to be genuine with others while being true to ourselves.

Our core information can change moment to moment. Each new situation, new person, and new interaction will tap new feelings, understandings, and interests. If we genuinely share core information in each moment, our energy is not trapped in black holes. It is not hidden from us, even though vulnerable feelings and secret understandings are released. Our core information, accepted and spoken aloud, allows our energy to flow into balance.

Core conversations are enhanced when we understand our own core information and also the core experiences of another. In the next chapter, you will learn how to help others find their core information by reflecting their energy. When you combine sharing your core information with helping others find their honest core information, core conversations are deeply satisfying and filled with expansive creative energy.

Core conversations move with life-force energy. They change and grow as new ideas and emotions are released into conversation. In core conversations black holes are acknowledged so they don't block the expression of core information, and energy is free to move into balance. Core conversations release creative energy, which is available to build your dreams and fulfill the passions of your soul.

Chapter Seven

Listening and Reflecting Energy

....

There was a woman called Bobbie who handled telephone complaints at the utility when I worked there. She told me about the following conversation with an angry customer who threatened to disrupt our rate hearing. After she talked to him, he came to the meeting, but instead of complaining he thanked us for helping him. His conversation with Bobbie is a great example of listening and reflecting energy.

───────── · · · · · ─────────

"They should hold a hearing before they raise rates like this. Some people can't afford to pay this much for electricity. I want to talk to the board," the customer shouted into the phone. "You're really irritated with us," said Bobbie.

"Yes, I am! That's why I called. This bill is twice what it was last month. Pretty soon I'll be paying more for electricity than for rent! I can't afford this!" "It really bothers you to have your bill go up so much," Bobbie said.

"It's more than that," the man said. "I don't know where I'll get the money and if you turn off my electricity, I can't do my work. I work at home on my computer. I'm just getting my business going and I don't have much income yet." "You need help instead of higher bills."

"I do. I can't be paying double for electricity. So, I demand to talk to the board." "You'd like to tell them to lower the rates," Bobbie said.

"That's what I want to do!" he agreed. "Is there anything else that you want?" Bobbie asked.

"I want you to reduce my bill and leave on the electricity until I get my business going." "You want to talk to the board, reduce your bill, and have electricity," Bobbie summarized. "Yes, that's what I want."

Once Bobbie understood what he was saying, she put him in touch with the energy management department. A person there showed him how to reduce his energy use and worked with his landlord to weatherize his home.

———— · · · · · ————

Listening for core information allows you to reflect the energy of what you hear. The secret is touching the core of what the other person is feeling, thinking, and wanting. When we reflect energy back this way, we acknowledge core information. We all have deeper layers of emotion and intention behind our superficial conversations, but our core motivations aren't always obvious. If we are skillful at reflecting energy, we can help each other understand the source of our words and actions. When we each understand our own core information, we have the power to discard our automatic pilot. Listening carefully is the secret.

Bobbie listened carefully to what the customer was saying. When she understood the emotion that was motivating him she reflected her understanding of his anger and then reflected his concerns. When the customer saw that his message had been understood, he could report his other concerns and interests. Finally Bobbie summarized what he wanted. When the customer realized that Bobbie understood how he felt, what it was about, and what he wanted, he was ready to find a solution.

With this skill, we can truly accept and understand each other. Core conversation begins with core information. Listening and reflecting is a way to help others find their core information. Practicing this kind of listening invites conversations to move to a more meaningful level and builds more satisfying relationships.

Listening by reflecting energy energizes others by attending to what they are saying. Our energy supports them in understanding their thoughts and feelings. The combined energy field we create together allows others to hear themselves and understand their own words. Listening and reflecting expands our collective understanding and illuminates deep personal truths. Sharing our core experiences in a field of acceptance is deeply connecting.

This reflective skill also protects us from pirating. Someone pirating energy may use anger, judgment, blame, guilt, withdrawal, humor, or upstaging us to steal our energy. Listening and reflecting deflects those energy pirating techniques and returns the energy to the sender. If the person is using blame and anger, that energy is deflected back to the person. If someone is judging us or making fun of us, we can mirror that energy back to him. If a person is ready to look into a self-revealing mirror, he may see himself in a new way. The mirror of listening and reflecting can move his energy away from us. Our own energy is protected behind a mirror of reflective energy.

Listening and reflecting taps and releases emotional energy. When someone gently acknowledges hidden emotion, energy and understanding are liberated. Listening and reflecting helps us understand our interests and desires, and helps us be more aware of what motivates us.

People skilled in reflecting energy feel energized by conversations that might trouble others—emotional conversations. They simply accept the feelings of the person they are listening to and have no agenda of their own to follow. They are not trying to change the person or make her feel or act differently. Through acceptance and acknowledgment they create an energy field of understanding and acceptance for what has been hidden. People who are effective listeners are comfortable with themselves. They are able to listen without needing approval or support. The more balanced a person's energy field the more acceptance and understanding she has for listening.

Listening and reflecting is built on a foundation of acceptance for what someone else is experiencing. Acceptance and understanding ease the release of blocked emotional energy. It is easier for us to accept and release our painful emotional memories when we are in an expanded accepting energy field. Personal energy is stored in our emotions. Acknowledging our emotions releases that energy.

Emotional energy can be blocked sequentially, as though stuffed into a pipeline. As one emotion is acknowledged and released, other emotions become accessible. Released personal energy is available for new choices, decisions, and actions. Our primary emotions are joy and fear. Expressing these emotions in all their forms releases energy. You may not realize that you have locked away natural emotions or interests. When someone close to you dies and you are unable to experience normal human grief and pain, part of your energy goes into protecting yourself from feeling it. If you yearn to move to a new job or community, but your family is solidly rooted, you may hide your desire from yourself. Soldiers who experience terror and tragedy in war hide their emotions because there is too much emotional energy to handle all at once. These experiences, hidden in our black holes, block our ability to listen and reflect energy effectively.

Shannon and Ted are married friends of mine who live in Portland, Oregon. They struggle with one issue repeatedly because Shannon's ability to listen is blocked with fear. She hasn't found a way to listen with acceptance to this one core issue. Ted, a rugged outdoorsman, loves to hunt and fish. He spends several weeks every year in Montana with "the boys" pursuing those activities. Ted would like to move to Montana. Shannon enjoys consulting with corporate clients in Portland and living in the city. Whenever Ted talks about how much he enjoys Montana, Shannon doesn't really hear or reflect on what he is saying because it triggers her fear that she would have to move away from her work and the city she loves. She isn't able to understand and reflect Ted's dream because listening to him triggers her fear. They lose precious connection with each other and both feel de-energized when they talk about Montana. Ted doesn't feel understood and Shannon feels scared that she'll have to choose between Ted and living in the city. Shannon and Ted are stuck. If Shannon were able to listen and reflect Ted's energy so that Ted felt understood, perhaps they would be able to work out a creative solution.

Shannon feeling threatened by Ted's love for Montana is an illustration of how other people's emotions and interests can trigger our own emotions. For example, do you feel angry or sad when someone is crying? Do you want him to stop? When you stumble into your own emotions, it's harder to stay open to someone else's core experience. You can become isolated in your own emotional turmoil. The skill of listening and reflecting is easier when you have released some of your black holes so that vulnerable emotions are less likely to be triggered. The following is an example of effective listening and reflecting. It shows what is possible when black holes don't get in the way.

——— • • • • • ———

Joan's sister Penny had been notified that the house she was renting had been sold and she had six weeks to move out. She called Joan in a panic, "I can't believe they sold my house. They didn't even tell me it was for sale. How can they do that?" Joan exclaimed, "Your house was sold!"

"Yes. They made this deal with Mark who rents the little house on the back of the lot. They sold him the whole lot including our house, and they never said a word to me. Now Mark wants to live in our house, and we have to move out." "You must be angry," Joan commented.

"Don't get me started. I'm in over my head at work again, and we're leaving on vacation next week. We've been thinking about buying a house, but all this is happening too fast." "You're under a lot of pressure," Joan reflected.

"Way too much. I didn't need this on top of everything else. I don't know where we're going to live." "You're worried about how this is all going to work out."

"I am! I really don't want to leave our house. I love it here. There's a garden and a separate studio out back next to Mark's house. The location is perfect. I don't know how we're going to find something this perfect." "It's been a great place," said Joan.

"And I don't have time to deal with all this stuff." "It seems overwhelming."

"It is. Usually I can do a lot, but this just seems like too much." "You expect a lot of yourself," observed Joan." "I do," admitted Penny.

"What do you want?" Joan asked. "We need a place to live." "Is there some way I can help?"

"Do you know a good realtor?" Penny asked. "Yes, I do. Let me get the number," Joan said.

Joan listened carefully so that she could reflect Penny's feelings. She also reflected the essence of the situation and found out what Penny wanted.

——————— · · · · · ———————

There are two ways of listening that do not reflect energy: automatic listening and problem solving listening. These are communication patterns that most of us use in normal conversation. They can keep us from connecting with each other and leave us vulnerable to energy pirating.

AUTOMATIC LISTENING

Automatic listening is based on the assumption that we already understand what another person is saying and have made up our minds about the matter. When someone enters into a conversation thinking the other person is wrong or confused and must be fixed, it leads to automatic listening. Automatic listening is not listening— it is reacting to what someone is saying, but hearing our own agenda. Some of us are busy preparing what we are going to say instead of listening. We are not really listening to his core experience. Instead, we listen for evidence of our preconceived assumptions, and upon hearing this evidence, we prepare for rebuttal. Then when it's our turn to speak (unless we interrupt first) we give him our prepared talk, often denying what he is saying and making suggestions to straighten him out. This technique is rarely satisfying for either person. The unconscious intention of automatic listening is to keep out new information and fix the other person.

Automatic listening has five characteristics: ignoring what the other person says, assuming we already know what she will say, interrupting her, denying her feelings, and wanting her to change. When I was growing up, I learned to rescue and fix other people. In my family when anyone was upset or troubled, everyone in the family assumed the job of fixing her—getting her to feel or behave differently. We were all so busy trying to change each other there was little time to look at our own problems.

I learned first to blame other people for making me feel uncomfortable, and then I busied myself in making them into better people. (Never mind that no one was interested in my suggestions!) It was a long time before I realized that I was pirating energy—self-righteous energy pirating. I wanted people to follow my rules of behavior. I assumed that I knew what was best for them, I pirated their energy by suggesting how they could change.

People adept at energy pirating are especially good at automatic listening. Energy pirates assume they are right, deny the way we look at things, interrupt us in the middle of the conversation, and basically ignore what we are saying. They want us to do things their way, either because they believe something is wrong with us or because we have triggered their black holes. Many times, however, these automatic conversations are subtler and superficially polite.

——————— • • • • • ———————

Automatic listening can seem fairly normal. I have two friends, Jim and Sandy, who are married. They found themselves caught in automatic listening, but have learned to listen to each other differently. Sandy lost her car keys often enough that Jim developed the habit of automatic listening. He assumed that she was not capable of keeping track of her keys. One morning when Jim was getting ready for work, Sandy raced into the bedroom where he was sitting on the bed tying his shoes. She opened the top drawer of the dresser, frantically searching through the underwear and scarves. Leaving the drawer half open, she rushed to the bathroom. Jim heard her opening and slamming shut drawers and cupboards. Emerging from the bathroom, she pleaded, "Jim, have you seen my keys? I've got an important meeting this morning at 8 o'clock, and I can't find them anywhere." Jim responded calmly, "If you would leave your keys in one place, like I do, we wouldn't go through this race to find the keys every week. Why don't you put your keys on the dresser at night? Then, they'd be there in the morning when you want them."

How well do you think Sandy liked Jim's response? Was she happy to have his suggestion? Did it give her energy or deplete her energy? Was Jim trying to fix Sandy? Was she broken? Sandy, afraid that she would miss the meeting, redoubled her efforts to find the keys. Now anger fueled her search. Eventually, she found her keys in the kitchen and left.

Jim wanted to correct Sandy's habit of losing her keys so he wouldn't have to help her find them, or find himself irritated by her habit. After their interaction, he knew that something was wrong. Her demeanor was icy from the moment he spoke until she left the house.

Jim was listening automatically (not listening) and responding according to his own assumptions. Automatic listening is like two ships passing in the night, wanting connection but not being able to achieve it. Automatic listening offers little chance for anyone to feel understood or acknowledged.

——————— • • • • • ———————

How many of us have listened to our children chattering, only half hearing what they were saying? We may have wished they would be quiet especially when we are tired or busy. Perhaps you have had the experience of a co-worker explaining something to you over and over. You may have felt irritated when she repeated herself, never realizing that she felt compelled to keep on talking until she felt understood. Automatic listening is a form of energy pirating—energy is lost in the exchange, energy that could be scooped up and poured into greater understanding.

Problem-Solving Listening

In the United States, we are good at listening in order to solve problems. We are a "can do" country and have built a great nation on solving problems. However, problem solving is not a good choice for every situation. In fact, problem-solving techniques that are used inappropriately are a form of energy pirating.

In automatic listening, we want to fix the person. In problem-solving listening, we want to fix the situation. All of us like coming up with our solution. There is a sense of satisfaction that we have accomplished something or helped someone. We have learned problem-solving techniques in school, at work, in volunteer activities: state the goal or problem; brainstorm alternative solutions; evaluate the options; and ask good questions.

When there is a problem, these tools serve us well, so well that we are tempted to use them to solve other people's problems even when they haven't asked us to. Men especially enjoy problem solving because they are good at it. It is usually the fathers' job to fix things around the house, so their sons also want to fix things and have been rewarded for doing so. Many women also lead with problem-solving skills. It was my problem-solving finesse that allowed me to climb the corporate ladder.

In listening to solve the problem, all questions are helpful. Leading questions are especially prized in the courtroom. Lawyers who win thrive on leading a witness through skillful questioning to preconceived conclusions. It may be hard for lawyers and others who are good at leading someone to a preconceived conclusion to listen for core information.

Skilled problem solvers are good at summarizing, probing, creating solutions, and advising. Someone listening to solve a problem listens to determine what advice to give. The listener scans his own life for familiar stories, and his response often arrives like this, "I had a problem like that once" or "I remember when we ran into something similar." Sometimes it is presented more straightforwardly, as in "Let me give you some advice." Advice can be helpful if you ask for it. It can even be interesting if you don't. Giving advice is especially tempting to problem solvers because they get energy from having their advice taken. They feel useful and wise—energizing themselves with the appreciation of others.

Someone with good problem-solving skills will be listening in order to clarify the problem, analyze the situation, probe for more information, question the facts, suggest solutions, evaluate alternatives, and give advice.

Many people ask for help in solving their problems and appreciate a little advice now and again. If someone isn't interested in having her problems solved, or if she is lost in her emotions and not ready for solutions, beware. Listening with the aim of solving problems is not really listening. It is scanning for information that fits the agenda of the problem solver. Problem-solving techniques can take over and change the agenda of the person speaking. If someone simply wants to be understood and doesn't want her problem solved for her, the listener who is looking for a problem to solve will be perceived as an energy pirate. Proceeding with your own agenda without considering the interests of another person is intimidator pirating.

While the problem solver feels energized by leading a problem-solving expedition, the person with the problem can feel misunderstood. It may be hard to talk a problem solver out of a solution we don't want. Dealing with an overzealous problem solver can deplete our energy and may lead us to think that we can't deal with our own problems. Most of us prefer to solve our own problems when we can. When we can't we can always ask for help.

The following stories give you an idea of the trouble we can get into if we jump into listening to solve the problem when it is not invited.

——————— • • • • • ———————

Paul was sitting at the breakfast table one morning when his wife, Linda, joined him, a serious look on her face. "Paul, I'm afraid I might have to sell Liza" (her name for her aging Volkswagen bug). Paul hated Liza. She was continually breaking down and Paul spent hours keeping her running. Overjoyed at the idea of getting rid of the car, he responded, "Great, I'll take it down to the mechanic and get the carburetor rebuilt and get the brakes fixed. Then I'll call in an ad for Saturday's paper. We'll have that thing out of here by Sunday."

How do you think Linda responded to Paul's listening to solve the problem? He listened and his agenda was to get rid of the car, fixing Linda's problem on the spot. She should be happy, right? Wrong! He missed a couple of clues. First of all, the car had a name, indicating that Linda had some attachment to Liza. Secondly, Linda didn't ask him to sell the car. She said she was afraid that she might have to sell her. Linda was feeling sad and reluctant. Paul didn't hear her core information.

After Paul responded, Linda felt angry and frustrated, but she didn't know why. Later that day when they had a chance to talk, Paul learned that the car was important to Linda because she drove it before they were married—part of the good times Linda and her single friends had in the city. Now they lived in the country, and Linda missed her friends.

Linda learned that Paul was frustrated trying to keep Liza operating. He learned what the car meant to Linda. Eventually they carried out Paul's original plan. They also made plans to visit the city and get together with Linda's old friends. Several hours of energy wasted on frustration, anger, and misunderstanding could have been prevented if Paul had truly listened to Linda at breakfast, heard her core experience, and connected with her by acknowledging it.

———— • • • • • ————

Here's another problem-solving situation. My friends Heather and Terry had just finished a year-long project that provided them both with temporary jobs at Hewlett-Packard. During the year they worked there they became close friends. Terry was packing up her office supplies when Heather walked in.

"You know, Heather," Terry said, sitting down, "I'm having a really hard time packing up this office." Heather answered, "No problem. The great part about working here is that we can call Facilities to help. They'll come over with boxes and pack it up for you. They do that all the time. Do you want me to give them a call?"

"Thanks, but that's not what I need right now. It's not really about the packing. I'm having a hard time because the project is coming to an end. I've made a lot of good friends here. I'm going to miss them.

I'm especially going to miss you, and I'm not sure what I'll do for a job after this." "Oh, Terry, I jumped right into problem solving because I don't want to feel sad about leaving, but I do. I'm really going to miss you, too."

Heather and Terry walked outside and talked for a while. They reminisced about the people they had grown to appreciate and the good times they'd had together. After Heather understood and acknowledged Terry's experience, Terry was ready to call Facilities and pack up.

Heather knew about problem solving and reflecting energy. She quickly realized that Terry didn't want help solving the problem and, in fact, hadn't asked for it. She switched to listening and reflecting.

Paul and Heather each had their own agenda. Paul's agenda was to sell Linda's car. As long as he proceeded on his agenda, he couldn't hear Linda or connect with her feelings. Heather's agenda was to help Terry feel better about the situation. When she realized that she could help best by listening, she stopped trying to solve the problem and began to listen for what Terry really wanted.

────── · · · · · ──────

When I want to test whether I'm problem solving or listening automatically, I ask myself whose agenda I'm pursuing. If my agenda is to improve the situation or help someone feel better, I am most likely problem solving. If my agenda is to help someone change so that I will feel better, I check for automatic listening. If I am genuinely curious about what someone wants, I may be listening and reflecting.

HOW TO LISTEN AND REFLECT ENERGY

Truly listening to another person does not mean agreeing with him. If you agree with someone that he has been wronged, you confirm that he is a victim and join him in blaming someone else. When you blame other people you are merely defending your black holes, even though you may feel connected in blaming. Listening and reflecting acknowledges feelings with acceptance and support without agreeing or disagreeing. It doesn't mean feeling sorry for someone, or arguing that he should be reacting differently or he should want something different. Arguing someone out of his feelings is useless. The more you try to convince him, the more he defends his stance verbally or nonverbally. On the other hand,

Here are some examples to give you some practice in distinguishing between agreeing, disagreeing, and reflecting. If Pat is looking for a job, which one of the following friends is giving him energy by actually listening to him, which one is pirating his energy by disagreeing and criticizing him, and which one joins him in blame?

Pat says: "I just got another rejection. Job hunting is really draining."

Friend 1: "How can they reject you?"

Friend 2: "Rejections are tough."

Friend 3: "You've got to get back out there and try harder."

The first friend agrees with Pat, confirming that he is a victim and he joins Pat in blaming the boss and questioning the rejection. This suggests there is little Pat can do to get what he wants. The hopelessness of not getting what he wants is an energy drain.

The third friend disagrees with Pat, criticizing him by suggesting that he should try harder. He implies that Pat hasn't done enough. This friend may be pirating Pat's energy by triggering his fear that he won't get a job. This friend may get energy from feeling slightly superior.

The second friend reflects Pat's core experience. The acknowledgment that "rejections are tough" suggests that this friend understands how Pat is feeling and what he is going through. This phrase implies acceptance, and energizes their relationship through connection.

Notice the differences in the responses in the next situation.

Randy says: "I'm struggling with this project, and they want it tomorrow."

Friend 1: "They really cut you short on time." (*Joining in blame*)

Friend 2: "If you hadn't wasted all that time, you'd be done by now." (*Pirating*)

Friend 3: "You're in a tough spot." (*Listening and reflecting*)

Listening and reflecting acknowledges another person's core feelings, thoughts, and wants. Most of us don't have much experience with this. We get little social encouragement to acknowledge our own emotions and intentions, let alone acknowledge what others are feeling. The first step in learning how to listen and reflect is to open a space inside ourselves for complete acceptance of another person's reactions, stories, and desires. Acceptance is not the same as approval. Accept that she knows her own situation best. Accept that we may or may not be able to help her. Accept that wherever she is is the right place for her to be. Accept that if we have a reaction to her core experience, then we have our own emotions to deal with.

Encountering someone's core experience may trigger one of our black holes. In the story about Joan's sister, Penny, Joan felt bad for her sister and wanted to help her find a place to live. But, if Joan had started talking about how bad she felt and slipped into a story about when she herself had been evicted, Penny wouldn't have had as much help in understanding her own core experience. Someone highly skilled in listening and reflecting will be able to set aside her own reactions for a short time in order to be a reflective mirror for someone else. Later she may want to expand the conversation by sharing her own core information. When we react to a person or a situation, we are not available to hear and accept what someone has to say. We are dealing with our own reaction instead of reflecting energy. If we can disengage from our own reaction and focus on what someone is saying, that's great. If we can't, we may need to name and acknowledge our own reaction to release it. Skillfully moving between sharing core information and listening and reflecting energy is the art of core conversation.

There are three ways to listen and reflect people's core

experience: guess how they are feeling; reflect their thinking; and ask what they want.

Guess How They Are Feeling

When you are talking with someone and you sense that she is feeling emotional, watch her eyes, body posture, and facial expression, and listen to the emotion in her voice. Then take your best guess at what she is feeling. It makes no difference if you guess wrong. By guessing an emotion you give the other person an incentive to go to her emotional state and check it out. She can then confirm or deny your guess. Whether you are right or wrong doesn't matter. What you are doing is helping her identify and claim her emotions and sensations.

If you guess a person is tense, he'll let you know if you're right. If you guess excited and he is feeling hyper, he will check in and claim some form of anxiety. If you guess sad and he is feeling rejected, he'll tell you that. If you guess angry and he is angry, but doesn't want to admit it, he may choose a word that takes the edge off his anger. "Not angry so much as concerned" or "unhappy," he may say. Your job is to help him name his emotions so you can both understand what is motivating him. If you get lucky or have a high level of skill and guess correctly, he will probably confirm your guess. Believe whatever he tells you. If it turns out to be the wrong word, he can correct it later.

This process works only if you use a word that describes a feeling, however. People often say they feel a thought. For example, "I *feel* like going downtown." "I *feel* that you are complaining." "I *feel* that you are making a big mistake." In these statements the word *feel* is followed by *like* or *that*. When *like* or *that* follows the word "feeling," the next phrase is almost always a thought. Complaining, going somewhere, and making a mistake are not feelings. They are thoughts. You could substitute *would* or *think* for *feel* and the sentence still sounds right. "I *would* like to go downtown." "I *think* you are making a big mistake." "I *think* you are complaining."

Guessing feelings works best when you limit your guess to one, two, or three words—the fewer the better. "Sounds very sad." "You're excited." "Seems troubling." Painful, huh?" Use your awareness to hit the center of their core emotional experience.

If there is a hint of insincerity or nonacceptance in your guess, the other person's defenses will go up. It is easy to lose the energy connection. For example, the statement "You sure seem angry to me" accuses him of anger rather than accepting that anger is his experience. The statement "You're just scared" has an element of judgment as if feeling scared isn't all right. Any guess tinged with accusation or judgment is disconnecting, rather than reflecting and connecting. One way to reflect anger or fear with acceptance is to say: "You seem angry," and "Are you scared?"

Once sensations and emotions are claimed, they change and evolve. Just as it's impossible to stay happy forever, it's also impossible to stay mad or hurt once these emotions are acknowledged and understood. Feelings are released as they are reflected. Freed emotions flow toward balance. Emotions and sensations remain stuck only if they are suppressed or blocked below the level of conscious awareness. So, in this process of guessing how the other person is feeling, accept whatever he comes up with as the truth of his experience and keep guessing as long as his countenance or voice shows emotion. Continue guessing until either one or both of you have acknowledged all your feelings.

Reflect Their Thinking

Reflecting people's thinking is also called paraphrasing, repeating their thoughts. I try to use different words so that people know I really do understand. Watch out for parrot phrasing, which can be perceived as mocking. For example, a friend says to you, "John took my idea and now they're giving him the credit," and you paraphrase, "I hear you say that John took your idea and now they're giving him the credit." Your friend may feel mocked rather than understood. The key to reflecting is to summarize the core of the situation without repeating her exact words. The core of the situation above is that your friend is not getting credit for her idea. Reflecting her thoughts is a way of helping your friend (or the "pirate" you are facing) see the truth of her situation. Don't be afraid to be wrong. Most people are happy to straighten you out as long as your efforts are sincere. If your reflection is not quite on target, they will describe the situation again. This gives you both a better understanding.

In the situation with Joan's sister, Penny, who had to move in six weeks, Joan paraphrased her situation, summarizing her thoughts. The phrase, "It's been a great place," reflects the value of her home to her and the acknowledgment that it is history. "You expect a lot of yourself," acknowledges Penny's belief that there is too much to deal with. Often people describe their situation so well you need only listen and be with them to convey that you understand. With deep connections, less verbal reflecting is needed.

Ask What They Want

The third part of listening and reflecting is to uncover interests and intentions. Once people have acknowledged their feelings and understand their situation, they are usually ready to move on to what it is they want. If you notice a pause for contemplation in the conversation, this may signal it's time to ask what they want.

"What do you want?" opens a door for them to discover their personal interests. You can be more specific and ask, "What do you want to do about..." In the conversation with her sister Penny, Joan asked simply, "What do you want?" She also could have said, "What do you want to do about a place to live?" This simple question hands the issue back to the speaker. The listener doesn't have to take on the speaker's dilemma. Energy pirates, thinking they know best, assume responsibility for the speaker's dilemma and try to solve it. That is, listening to solve the problem as described above.

If the speaker pauses to consider the question, "What do you want?" your timing is perfect. If he cycles back into his feelings, continue to accept and acknowledge all his feelings. Honor his insight as he talks about how everything fits together and ask again later what it is he wants. Eventually, he will feel complete and know what he wants to do.

Listening and reflecting conversations often end with the

understanding of what the person wants. Once emotions and intentions have been heard, however, the person may be interested in having you help him solve the problem. Ask if he would like your help. He may want your advice or thoughtful questions on how to achieve his intent. Problem solving, if invited, can be helpful after listening and reflecting.

——————— · · · · · ———————

Let's take another look at Penny's situation to see how all the parts fit together. Joan's sister Penny had been notified that the house she was renting was being sold and she had six weeks to move out. She called Joan in a panic. "I can't believe they sold my house. They didn't even tell me it was for sale. How can they do that?" "Your house was sold!" Joan exclaimed. (*Reflecting her thinking*)

"Yes. They made this deal with Mark who rents the little house on the back of the lot. They sold him the whole lot including our house, and they never said a word. Now Mark wants to live in our house, and we have to move out," "You must be angry," Joan commented. (*Guessing her feelings*)

"Don't get me started. I'm in over my head at work again, and we're leaving on vacation next week. We've been thinking about buying a house, but all this is happening too fast." "You're under a lot of pressure." (*Guessing her feelings*)

"Way too much. I didn't need this on top of everything else. I don't know where we're going to live." "You're worried about how this is all going to work out." (*Guessing her feelings*)

"I am! I really don't want to leave our house. I've loved it here. There's a garden and a separate studio out back next to Mark's house. The location is perfect. I don't know how we're going to find something this perfect." "It's been a great place," said Joan. (*Reflecting her thinking*)

"And I don't have time to deal with all this stuff." "It seems overwhelming." (*Guessing her feelings*)

"It is. Usually I can do a lot, but this just seems like too much." "You expect a lot of yourself," observed Joan. (*Reflecting her thinking*) "I do," admitted Penny.

"What do you want?" Joan asked. (*Asking about her wants*) "We need a place to live." "Is there some way I can help?" (*Invitation to solve the problem*)

"Do you know a good realtor?" Penny asked." "Yes, I do. Let me get the number," Joan said.

You'll notice that the listening and reflecting does not always proceed in order as steps 1, 2, and 3. Most people mix their feelings in with their thoughts as they talk. The listener follows the speaker. Wants usually come closer to the end of a core conversation, but not always. Sometimes people cycle back into their feelings or think of other things after acknowledging what they want.

———— · · · · · ————

The next story is a conversation I had with my friend, Jack. As you read this conversation, notice that I used three different ways of listening and reflecting: my guessing his feelings, my reflections on his thinking, and my question about what he wants. Notice when the conversation moves into problem-solving questions.

"First, they want my resignation," said Jack. "Now, they've asked me not to tell anyone that I'm leaving because I was pressured out of my job. They want me to lie. They're blackmailing me with a severance package. They are saying that if I tell the truth about this, they'll pull the package." "So they want your head on a platter and they want you to put it there yourself so they don't have blood on their hands?" I offered.

"That's it exactly. The network is afraid that if my staff knows the truth it will create a backlash in the newsroom. The news staff is loyal to me, but the new president wants me out." "It's a tough setup," I acknowledged.

"I hate it. I feel so compromised. They've got me over a barrel. If I don't cooperate, I don't know how I'll put my kids through college for another year. My stomach turns every time one of my staff asks me if I'm looking forward to retirement." "You're sick about this."

"I am. They're forcing me to pretend with the people I care the most about. I don't know what to do. I don't know what to say." "You're angry," I guessed.

"I've got a right to be angry," he confirmed. "You're not getting what you want," I reflected.

"No. I want this to all go away. I want my job back. I want to walk back into the newsroom and plan how to cover Congress, the Balkans, and the Middle East. I don't want the network president influencing how we cover the news. Political influence has no place in the newsroom," Jack emphasized. "You love your job," I reflected.

"I really care about what gets reported and the people who work their hearts out to get it right night after night. And I'm damn good at it too. You know, we won four national awards and doubled our viewing audience in the eight years I managed the news." "You're proud of what you've done and they can't see it. That hurts."

"Boy, does it. The president says I'm not a team player. What does that mean? That I don't do it his way." "The president wants to run the news his way, and you want to run it your way."

"Yeah, but my way is the right way." "It must seem so after all those awards and the vote of confidence from the viewers," I acknowledged.

"Why can't he see that?" Jack asked. "That's a good question. Why can't he?"

"He has a different agenda. He takes the viewers and awards for granted. He wants his people to have the prestigious visible roles. He's telling me who to feature and what news to air." "Sounds like an impossible situation," I acknowledged.

"I can't stay with that kind of interference. I just wish they would recognize all I've done for them." "You've worked your heart out for the network."

"I have. I don't think anyone could have done a better job." "No one could have done a better job." I confirmed.

"This is miserable," Jack said. "It must be very hard. What do you really want?"

"It is really hard. I'm used to having things go my way, but under the circumstances, I guess it is my choice to leave. And with the severance package, I'll be able to put my kids through school." "Your kids are really important to you."

"I've got great kids and Kate [his wife] is being incredibly supportive." "You have good support."

"I do, and my staff has been very supportive. I just don't know what to tell them." "Saying good-bye is hard to do. What will you say to them?" I asked.

"I have to tell them that it's hard to leave. But, I can also tell them that together we did a great job, that I care about them, and that I'm looking forward to working on my book." "Does that feel right?" I asked. "It doesn't feel good, but it feels right."

Jack wanted me to help him understand how he felt about the situation and decide what to do. I reflected information so he could release his feelings and find his interests. I didn't give him anything new to consider—he had all the information he needed to know what to do. I helped him by guessing that he was sick and angry about what was happening, that he was proud and loved his job, that he felt hurt, and that it was very hard. I reflected his situation, "They want your head on a platter, you're not getting what you want, the president wants to run the news his way, no one could have done a better job, your kids are important to you, and you have good support." After he acknowledged that he felt miserable, I asked him what he really wanted. Later we switched to problem solving when I asked, "What will you say to them [his staff]?"

Once Jack understood his core information—his feelings, thoughts, and wants—he took action to move toward what he wanted, given the situation. The conversation with Jack lasted an hour. Listening and reflecting can also take place easily and quickly—a shorthand way of gaining understanding and deciding what to do.

——————— · · · · · ———————

Here is another example of listening and reflecting. This is a much shorter conversation. Listening and reflecting is used only once to create agreement on the action.

Pat and Jerry were sitting on the floor at the side of the room where we were holding a workshop. The rest of the participants were in rows of chairs in the middle of the room. The workshop leader asked everyone to move his chair into a large circle. As the chairs were being reformed into a circle, and chairs were placed in front of Pat and Jerry, they continued to sit on the floor.

Gary noticed the two on the floor and said, "Come on you guys, get a chair and join the circle." Pat reflected his emotion. "You must be uncomfortable that we are sitting on the floor."

Gary stopped to check his experience and responded, "No, I'm uncomfortable sitting in front of you." The three of them rearranged the chairs so that Pat and Jerry could be on the floor and in the circle.

——————— · · · · · ———————

Any time someone is upset with you or troubled by something you've done, listening and reflecting is the best way to use your energy. Listening and reflecting deflects any hooks that might snag your energy and drag you into supporting others energetically. Most people, even when pirating, can be encouraged to greater understanding through listening and reflecting. Unless there is a history of dysfunction in the relationship, acknowledging someone's core truth takes the intensity out of his reaction, but only if offered with genuine curiosity and openness.

The following are pirating comments and reflective responses that deflect the energy with acceptance and understanding.

This job is a waste of time(Pirating). You don't like what you're doing(Listening and reflecting).

You should have given me a better grade(Pirating). You're disappointed with your grade(Listening and reflecting).

I'm not upset, do whatever you want, just like you always do(Pirating). You're unhappy with the way I handle things(Listening and reflecting).

You are controlling and manipulative(Pirating). You're troubled by something I've said or done(Listening and reflecting).

Did I interrupt you in the middle of my sentence(Pirating)? Sounds like you have more to say(Listening and reflecting).

When someone is upset with you and you openly guess his feelings, he will settle into one of two responses. He will either like the connection to his truth and settle down for more conversation, or he won't like it and avoid you because listening and reflecting is powerful, and he doesn't know how to respond. Listening and reflecting keeps you open to the truth of others and centered in yourself. When you reflect energy, however, you let go of the need to change others and focus instead on developing listening and reflecting skills as the best way to maintain your energy around pirating.

The key is acceptance that others are doing the best they know how to live their lives fully and well. They have patterns that work for them. They have survived the challenges of life because of their pirate strategies. We can protect our energy and help others see their pirate strategies by naming their core feelings and intentions. Then they have a choice that comes from greater understanding if they want that kind of illumination.

Listening and reflecting deflects energy pirating, but if our purpose is to change the person pirating energy, then we are also pirating. If instead our purpose is to reflect energy so that we can both understand, then we may be helping him. With this clarity people can choose to change their behavior when dealing with us, or they may discover a pattern they want to change. Any choice they make is theirs, including the choice to remain unchanged. With listening and reflecting we act as a mirror for clarity, accepting their choices whatever they may be. If we learn to listen and reflect together, we can have deeply meaningful core conversations. Core conversations weave back and forth from core sharing to listening and reflecting. From these meaningful conversations we can gain insight into others we care about and ourselves. Core conversations are a life-long practice. We don't get finished one time and we're done. Every new moment is an opportunity to discover and understand others and ourselves more deeply. The best we can do is be true to ourselves and reflect what we see and hear from others.

We may want to practice with close friends or family members so that we can support each other. The energy connection that comes from core conversations is powerful. Connection allows us to get to the core of an issue and know what we want at a soul level. The energy generated from core conversations is not only deeply satisfying—it is also life giving and highly creative.

Listening and reflecting is a gift. By listening in this way we offer acceptance, understanding, and clarity. We do not judge or try to change people. We do not take on their problems and try to solve them. We are not on automatic pilot, reacting to what we thought was said. We are fully present, searching for the core meaning of what someone is saying. This gift of understanding is powerful and rare. When we truly feel accepted and understood it touches us deeply.

Chapter Eight

Balancing and Aligning Energy

....

As we release our black holes and balance our energy fields, life-sustaining energy fills us. When we listen and connect with others, our creative energy expands. There is a source of energy that expands and fills us, that feeds our life force, and sweeps us into life. Eastern religious philosophies call this energy chi. The more chi we have, the more our energy fields flow with creative energy. Life force energy may account for the survival of some individuals under conditions in which most living beings perish. Some of us live through seemingly impossible experiences. Many return home with harrowing and unbelievable stories. Of those who are diagnosed with cancer, some follow standard medical prognoses while others return to full, healthy, productive lives. How do these survivors endure against biological odds? What is the source of energy that sustains them? How do survivors call on this source of energy?

We are born with life force energy. If you have been with someone near death, you may have experienced the loss of his spirit, his life force. At the moment of death, his spirit leaves. His body remains, but the person you knew is gone. Our life force infuses our bodies with awareness. That life force is the seer, the one who watches us do what we do, the one who recognizes our mental activity as thought. Your observer is thinking about this idea right now. The observer of our thoughts, emotions, intentions, and actions is our life force, our soul. I think of our soul and life force as one and the same. Our life force animates and magnifies our energy fields. When some of our life force energy is sucked into black holes, we feel tired and depressed or even become physically ill. We are not as open to the flow of life-giving energy.

I believe there is a universal "Source." When we tap into that Source, we energize our life force, our energy fields, and our creative energy. We can balance and expand our life force without pirating energy from others. This Source is one presence and one power that permeates conscious life. There are many names for this energy source—Allah, Brahman, Buddha, Creator, Deepest Wisdom, Dharmakaya, Gaia, God, Highest Guidance, Holy Spirit, Infinite Source, Keter, Li, Rigpa, Tao, and Yahweh, to name a few. There are many spiritual paths. The name you use is a personal choice.

Currently, spiritual seekers are learning from many religious perspectives. We are becoming aware that the underlying principles in the world's major religions are similar. A basic common element in most religions is a belief in one source of power, one supreme presence of spirit that supports life. For me, the Source of life force energy is a presence that embodies all of creation. This presence is an energy field of infinite possibilities. I believe we are part of this infinite field; a conscious, intelligent part of this presence, choosing and directing our creative energies.

How we live our lives directly influences how much life force we have. Our thoughts, emotions, and behaviors determine how much life force energy flows through our personal energy fields. With Source energy, I believe it is possible to renew our spirits and nourish our souls to be more fully alive, healthy, and fulfilled.

I feel humbled by attempting to suggest how to do this. I am the first to admit that we have much to learn about human energy fields and life force energy. Our personal life force is not constant or discrete. Energy flows in and out of our personal energy fields, converting from energy to matter and back again. Some of us are filled with energy and love for mankind. Some of us are not aware of our energy fields. Most of us experience times when we feel fully alive and other times when we feel disconnected and drained. These experiences correspond to the fullness and flow of our personal energy field. We use terms and phrases such as energized, empowered, disempowered, gave my power away, running on empty, tired, drained, and full of energy. These phrases help us express the balance and flow of our life force energy.

As I mentioned earlier, I call life force energy "Source." You may prefer another term for the presence of energy and life, perhaps one of the ones I mentioned above. Use a name that is comfortable for you. I believe that Source energy forms our energy fields, and that all living beings are part of one giant fluid energy system. We are all a part of Source. I believe that unseen spiritual forces guide and protect us. Some call these energy forces "spiritual guides" or "guardian angels." When I call on Source, unseen spiritual energy forces respond. I am able to request and receive spiritual support because I am connected to and part of the Source. If Source were an ocean, each of us would be a wave, flowing separately, yet connected. I believe that we are separate manifestations of Source energy. We have individual awareness, but we are part of and empowered by the Source.

Receiving Source energy is like breathing. As fresh air flows freely into healthy lungs, so Source energy flows freely into healthy energy fields. Having black holes in our energy fields is like having black lung disease. With black holes, Source energy is partially blocked. Black holes impede the flow of Source energy like diseased lungs suffocating in the presence of fresh air. So, too, can energy pirating close down an energy field. People pirating energy tend to withhold and protect their energy instead of being openly accepting of others. A protected energy field constricts the flow of Source energy in the field, just as air polluted with smog or smoke makes breathing more difficult. If you participate in a field characterized by pirating and protection, opening to Source energy is risky. It requires more effort from you than if you were in an energy field where people openly accept each other.

Source has no beginning, no end. Source energy is constantly flowing and always available, never used up. We must close it off with our black holes. When we release a black hole we can feel our energy expand. Once black holes are released, Source energy fills us and empowers our intentions.

Source energy is like hydroelectricity. A flowing river turns electric turbines. As generating turbines whirl, electricity is spun into transmission lines. Substations and transformers step this energy down in voltage to be used in homes and businesses. Even though the river flows continuously, and electric generators are constantly in motion, no energy flows into our homes until we flip the switch. When we turn on the switch, electricity flows in.

In order for electricity to flow through transmission lines, there must be a use for the energy at the consumer end of the line—heat, light, an appliance or computer. Electricity will not flow through a transmission line unless it is being used at the end of the line. Unlike water in a pipe, electricity can't be stored in the line. It must have somewhere to go. Electricity flows as it is used. More generators come on line in the morning as the electric load, the amount being used, increases. When the system is not in balance—when more electricity is being generated than used—as sometimes happens in storms, overloaded transformers can burn up and generators automatically shut down as the system adjusts to changes in flow. In every moment, the amount of electricity generated equals the amount of electricity in use (plus a minimal amount lost in transmission). Electricity generated is always in balance with electricity in use.

Source energy is also in balance with our capacity to switch on and use life force energy. When we use energy—moving, working, talking, playing, creating—more Source energy flows through us. The more energy we use and the more open to Source we are, the more our life force expands. When our emotions flow freely, we have capacity for more Source energy. When our energy field is free of black holes, we draw more life force energy. When our energy field is aligned, energy flows more easily.

This book suggests many ways to balance and expand our life force energy. Releasing black holes and energy pirating, connecting to others through core conversations, are the primary ways I have talked about. There are four additional practices and four energy principles that influence our openness to Source energy. These practices are alignment, meditation, spending time in natural environments, and synergy. Alignment orders our internal experience and actions with integrity. Meditation opens our awareness to Source. Spending time in natural environments refreshes our life force energy. Synergy expands our energy fields through connection with others. The four principles govern Source energy and human energy fields.

ALIGNMENT

Aligning our energy fields requires that we pay attention to integrity and agreements. Integrity is aligning our formative information— our thoughts, emotions, and intentions—with our words and actions. When our intentions and our words are connected to and consistent with our actions, we create more flow. If you have four horses connected to a wagon, you're not going very far until you get them lined up and going in the same direction. The same is true when our emotions and intentions are aligned with our words and actions. When we are true to ourselves and true to what we agree to do, we have integrity. Integrity aligns our fields and expands our life force energy.

Integrity opens the flow of Source energy to grow and strengthen our life force. Turning on a toaster draws electrical current through the household wiring, which pulls current through the transmission line that draws electricity through the transformer from the generator. Similarly, thoughts, emotions, intentions, words, and actions draw life force energy through our energy fields. Integrity allows Source energy to expand and flow freely.

We affect the flow of life force energy with everything we think, feel, and do. Just like flipping the switch for electric current, we can draw more creative energy into our field. Keeping our agreements smoothes the way for Source energy. People who understand the effect of broken agreements are careful to follow through with what they say they will do. Every broken agreement, no matter how small, leaves misaligned energy and weakens the flow of life force energy. Keeping agreements and maintaining integrity is not for others to judge—it is for us to know. Integrity is being true to ourselves when no one else knows. By honoring our agreements we respect and honor another person as well as ourselves. Honoring our agreements creates safety in the collective energy field, which opens the field to a greater flow of Source energy.

Ken and Marie had been together for almost 25 years. After some time they gave up hope of ever having children. But there was a miracle and a son came to them, who was the focus of their relationship. Marie didn't resent Ken's job which included a lot of traveling. She had a business at home that she loved and she appreciated that she didn't have to cater to Ken much. Ken loved Marie and his son, but wished she were more affectionate.

Ken's work took him to Europe and South America as well as across the U.S. and back. When Ken traveled, he felt attracted to other women and occasionally spent the night with one. He never told Marie about this and justified his actions by telling himself that a slight sexual indiscretion had nothing to do with his marriage. But Ken was out of alignment with himself. He had lost his integrity and his energy because of the disconnection between his marriage vows and his actions. He had broken his agreement with himself, his wife, and his son.

Source energy is disconnected where there are broken agreements. There are four basic levels of agreements. All levels include agreements with people at work, family and friends, and agreements with ourselves.

The first level of agreement is when we say we will do something we don't really intend to do. For example, if I run into you on the street, we might chat for a few minutes. At the end of our conversation, you might say, "Let's get together some time." To be polite, I might agree. We have been taught to be polite, to hide our truth so as not to hurt other people's feelings. Yet, there is a small piece of my attention—my energy—that knows my words and actions aren't lined up, aren't aligned.

Sam is an easygoing man in his mid-twenties. Since college, he works as a river rafting guide in the summer and a ski lift operator in the winter. He scrapes by, living in friends' rental units or crashing at his parents' house between jobs. Everyone loves Sam. He's concerned about other people and is a good listener. If he says he'll help you out, you can count on him. He fits in almost anywhere.

In the summer he buys river rafting gear from the river outfitter, and in the winter he buys ski gear. He buys at wholesale rates, but Sam never quite makes enough money to pay for all the gear he buys. He has several credit cards that are maxed out. He intends to pay them off, but he never gets enough ahead to pay more than the interest. He tells himself that he should stop buying gear, but it's too tempting. Sam lacks integrity. He has not been true to his intention to stop buying gear or to pay off his credit cards. His energy suffers each month as his debts grow.

Kevin said he'd call and then forgot. Wendy agreed to get to work on time, but was late more often than not. Terry promised herself she'd stop eating so many sweets, but didn't. Lori told herself she'd run three days a week, but only managed to get out one weekend a month. Brian promised himself he'd stop smoking and kept lighting up. Frank wanted to cut down on alcohol, but somehow didn't get around to it.

These are all well-meaning people. Each lost energy when he didn't intend to follow through with what he said he wanted. When words don't align with actions, the agreements have been broken. They were breaking their agreements with themselves. When we don't follow through on agreements, we hurt ourselves, and the ultimate price we pay is the loss of our life force energy.

The same is true of our agreements with others. In addition to the cost to ourselves, we lose acceptance, responsibility, and freedom. I have a colleague who works with teenagers. He tells the teens that keeping their agreements is the most important way to increase their freedom. The more they can build trust with their parents by following through on their agreements, the more their parents will stop trying to control their behavior. The connection between agreements and freedom is also true for the rest of us.

Examples of level one agreements may include paying off your credit cards, cleaning the garage, cleaning out the kitchen cupboards, calling or writing relatives, getting your taxes done earlier, sorting through the desktop on your computer screen, looking for a new job, recycling the junk mail—the list of personal unfulfilled intentions is usually long. Each one of these agreements requires a speck of your attention. When the list is long, your life force energy may be stagnating.

I encourage you to write a list of the things you have promised yourself you would do. Then start doing something about them. It may mean hiring your son to help you with the garage, hiring a cleaning service to clear the clutter out of the house. It may mean renegotiating the time when these things will get done or canceling some agreements with yourself. Or it may mean just doing it. You will be surprised by how much energy you have to tackle something on your list once you intend to do it. When you have completed the list—finished all your projects—you will feel more energized.

A level two agreement is when we intend to do something and say we will do it, but may not get it done. For example, we run into each other on the street and have a delightful conversation. At the end, I suggest that we get together sometime to continue our conversation. We both would like to see each other. We exchange cards. Will this meeting take place? Maybe yes, maybe no. There is no definite time or expectation that a commitment has been made.

Level two agreements also include agreements with people who have a habit of not following through. Do you know people like that? When they say they will do something, you know there's a good chance it won't happen. Or if it does, it will be quite a bit later than your original expectation. The first time this happens you are concerned or surprised. The second time you are frustrated. By the third time, you have adjusted your expectations and either form your plans around their inconsistencies or withdraw your trust. You may not give them any more responsibility or choose to deal with them again.

Brad is a fun-loving guy. He works construction when he can get a job. I asked him if he would replace several support beams under the deck of my house. Brad was polite on the phone and promised to come over within a week to bid on the job. Several weeks went by and Brad didn't come. I called him again. He apologized and said he'd be over in the next couple of weeks. When I called him a third time several weeks later, he assured me that this was unusual and he'd be over any day now. He did come about two weeks later and made a reasonable bid. I knew that a speedy job was unlikely, but the job wasn't critical and I wanted to see exactly how long it would take Brad to fix my deck. Realizing that I could not count on Brad, I called him every month or so to check on his plans. The deck was finished nine months later. It was professionally done and not very expensive.

Brad's action was out of alignment with his words. Because he lacked integrity, his energy was compromised. It was not surprising that he had little time to do the things he really wanted to do. Misalignment is common in energy fields. When Source energy flows through conflicting thoughts, emotions, intentions, words, and actions, the flow of Source energy is restricted in this maze.

If you are a person who makes level two agreements, you have probably experienced other people's irritation and resulting loss of trust, along with your loss of a sense of responsibility and connection. These are the prices we pay for level two agreements. If our words and actions don't line up, the result may be self-doubt, low self-respect, and loss of self-trust. Keeping our agreements builds trust and belief in ourselves. As with other broken agreements, however, the greatest price we pay is loss of life force energy.

Level three agreements are intentions with a solid commitment. With a level three agreement, when I say I will call you, I do. When we agree to meet for lunch, we set a time and a place, and you can count on me to be there, on time and ready for lunch. At level three, my word is my bond. At this level, I make no agreements unless I fully intend to do whatever is necessary to keep them. I align my intentions, my words, and my actions. This high level of alignment opens my personal energy flow and brings forth a higher level of Source energy.

There are two permissible occasions when it is okay to break a level three agreement. First, if I run into a difficulty, I let you know and renegotiate my agreement. At level three, I fully intend to follow through. I renegotiate rarely, only if serious unforeseen circumstances arise, and I let you know with as much advance warning as possible. I stay engaged with you until a satisfactory alternative is set up. The second exception to the level three agreement is what I call a profound agreement. A profound agreement is being true to my family and myself. For example, if I have an agreement to meet you at 3p.m., and at 2:30 my son's school calls to let me know that he has broken his arm, I have a profound agreement to be there. I may not have time to let you know and renegotiate a time for us. When I have to choose between a level three agreement and a profound agreement, the level three agreement is broken. Later when I contact you, I let you know what has happened and renegotiate our agreement.

A level three agreement means you can count on me to be there and provide what we agreed upon. On the rare occasion when I want to change some part of our agreement, you can count on me to contact you and stay engaged with you until you feel satisfied with any changes. This level of agreement opens the flow of life force energy. There are no unfulfilled agreement snags in your energy field to puzzle the flow of Source energy.

A level four agreement is the highest level of agreement. I sometimes call this a Zen agreement. At this level, if you agree, it is as good as done. In *Star Trek*, Captain Picard expects a level four agreement when he says, "Make it so." Only people with expansive energy fields can make level four agreements. They have such a command of the flow of their creative energy and their integrity is so powerful that what they say they will do, they do. Their thoughts, emotions, intentions, words, and actions create their reality. Level four agreements are rare, but there are some spiritually expansive beings who make only level four agreements. Since these agreements are unusual, I offer a fable as an example.

The story takes place in a village in Poland during World War II. Every Tuesday, like clockwork, the villagers count on the egg man to bring a basket of eggs to each house in the village. When soldiers came into the village one day, the villagers hid in their homes. One woman crawled under the bed with her two children and kept them quiet. She heard gunfire and shouting on the street outside her home. She didn't know where her husband was. She was terrified and panic-stricken. In a lull in the gunfire, there was a knock at the door. She lay in terror under the bed and didn't move. The knock came again. She put a finger to her lips. Her eyes begged her children's silence. The third time she heard the gentle rapping at her door, she wondered if it was news of her husband. She scooted out from under the bed and crept to the front door. She peeked through a crack in the door and saw the egg man. She opened the door just enough to pull the egg man inside and quickly shut the door.

"What are you doing?" she asked in disbelief.

"It's Tuesday," he said, "I brought your eggs."

MEDITATION

Meditation also helps open our energy fields to the flow of life force energy. People who have thought of meditating, but don't have a regular practice, have their reasons. "Meditation seems like nothing is happening. How can that help?" "I don't have time for it in my busy schedule." "My mind just won't quiet down, so I don't get much out of it." "I should meditate and I intend to do it more regularly in the future."

I also had all these reasons before I understood the gift of meditation. It's not the same as contemplation or prayer. In meditation, you are strengthening your observer-self. Your observer is part of your soul, the infinite part of you that is always present. You may or may not be aware of it. Meditation allows you to become familiar with your spiritual energy. When you are quietly centered in your spiritual energy field, you will notice the nudges from your spiritual guides. If you would like more spiritual guidance in your life, meditation is a way of increasing that connection and awareness.

I recommend meditating for 20 minutes once or twice a day. Meditation seems easier on an empty stomach. First thing in the morning is a good time. Sit in a comfortable position. Choose a favorite chair or sit upright in the middle of your couch or on the floor. Place your feet flat on the floor or fold your legs under you, whichever is more comfortable for you. Lay your hands comfortably in your lap. Make sure you are warm enough; use a blanket if your house is cool. Breathe deeply at first to relax, then breathe comfortably. Be aware of your own physical presence and any body sensations. Notice your breathing and the thoughts in your mind. Name each thought in your mind. You might say to yourself, "the kids, work problems, breathing, worrying, lost in thought." When you notice that you are contemplating, or hoping, or praying, or feeling emotional instead of observing, just name it and continue to observe and be aware of your physical sensations. That's all there is to it. You are developing awareness of your thoughts, emotions, and desires. In between, your body may feel moments of empty space. You may not notice the space for a while. No matter, it is there and at some point you will have a momentary awareness of it. The spaces around your thoughts, emotions, and intentions give you a sense of peaceful energy. At first, your mind may be filled with busyness. That's all right. Just notice your breathing. With practice, you will get better at naming and noticing your experience.

This evening I meditated on my favorite beach as the sun sank toward the Pacific Ocean. I sat in my purple camp chair at the entrance to a small cave. I recorded my experience to share with you. This was what I noticed in my meditation. Heart beating... breathing... ocean roar... dripping water... searching for thought... smiling at myself for searching... twinge in my back... breeze on my face... golden opaque color... waiting... tickle on my foot... energy expanding inside my head... deep breath... head turning right... head turning left... brightness in front of my face... smiling... relaxing... ironing board in a closet... warmth of sun on my legs... dripping... ocean roar... fear of someone approaching... heart beating faster... breathing faster... warmth of the sun on my face... energy expanding in my chest... back twinge... talking with a friend about death... sadness... a golden rock on my bedroom carpet... golden light through my eyelids... a sigh... the breeze... tingle in my left arm... sleepy... twinge in my back... shift in my chair.

In meditation, I am fully present to and yet slightly detached from my moment-to-moment experience. When you detach from and accept your thoughts and feelings, you are observing from your soul. This deep connection opens your field to the flow of Source energy. I do this by observing and accepting my experience, whatever it is. As you practice, you will gain comfort in accepting your thoughts and emotions. You may never empty your mind, but the chatter will gradually slow down.

Set up your meditation so that you won't need an alarm. Have someone come into the room or develop your own internal clock. A peaceful ending allows your awareness and spiritual connection to stay with you longer. If you would like more help, take a class or find someone who meditates regularly to support you as you get started.

SPENDING TIME IN NATURAL ENVIRONMENTS

Natural environments refresh and renew our energy, and help us leave the stress of our working lives behind. But they do even more for us. There is a presence of Source energy that infuses natural environments. An undisturbed sense of peace and serenity enfolds us as we open and relax—hiking among trees, sitting by a stream, camping out, walking on the beach. I believe there is a balance with nature that is essential to our well-being. I am concerned that we may not notice or value this important balance until we have disturbed and developed too much of our beautiful planet.

I encourage you to explore natural environments near you and frequent your favorite places regularly to renew and refresh your spirit. Even a walk in the park can give you a sense of flow and evenness that is hard to find in the normal routine of your day.

Those of us who have experienced the euphoria of climbing a mountain, the thrill of running a river, the power of sailing the ocean know this sense of place, this balance. We are a part of something wondrous and magnificent. Our natural environment reminds us of this and seeps into our spirit in ways we don't understand. Without this experience, we lose a part of ourselves. We lose a sense of who we are. We lose the clarity of our connection to Source energy.

Source is in and of everything. We need only study a wild rose. Taste a wild blackberry. Raise our eyes to the wonder of a sunset-colored madrone. Gaze at light shafts filtering through a deep forest. Await the green flash of a perfect sunset on the ocean. Marvel at the eclipse of the sun. Wonder at a sky filled with thousands of twinkling lights. Be awakened by the silver flashes of waves summoned by a full moon across the water. Watch a gray wolf trot silently through camp or a golden grizzly and her two cubs lope across the tundra. Feel the warmth of the spring sun on our faces and remember there is wonder in every wildflower, and magnificence in every living being. Nature reminds us that we are a part of this magnificence, this energy, this timeless beauty. Nothing manmade can replace this natural sense of wonder.

An untold amount of stress, weariness, concern, pain, drudgery, worry, and heaviness can be lifted and balanced with nature. We need only take the time and make the effort to seek the glen, the park, the estuary, the forest, the stream near us to regularly renew and refresh our sense of ourselves, and our core energies. Whenever you sense too much tension, approach the breaking point, or feel as though you are drowning in a black hole, move through your natural environment. Surrender to natural forces, and allow yourself to be held in a refreshing shower of Source energy that is constantly flowing and available.

SYNERGY

Groups are even more powerful than individuals in drawing and directing spiritual energy. Groups that align their beliefs, intentions, and actions call forth Source energy. This focused, expanded energy is called synergy. Synergy is the powerful flow of Source energy, lifting a group beyond what individuals alone, even at their best, can do. The group doesn't have to be large for synergy to happen. A group is two or more people. Two or more people can expand their thinking perspectives and creativity exponentially more than one alone. Two or more can release an expanded field of creativity. When expansive creative energy is unleashed, a group produces results far greater than the sum of the contributions of each member.

When groups function at this level, they become magnets for

resources and energy. A flow of creative, productive, joyful energy is evident in the results. An example of group synergy is a choir whose combined voices blend so beautifully that the audience is overcome with emotion. When an orchestra creates synergy, we can feel the music in our bodies. In fact, sometimes music can help unlock our black holes. Some music seems heavenly inspired— perhaps it is.

Unfortunately, most groups are sucked into patterns that stymie their fulfillment and creativity instead of creating synergy. At work, most people withhold their full energy and participation. Few are willing to be open and genuine about their core feelings, thoughts, and wants. Groups form argumentative and unproductive patterns instead, allowing energy pirating to dominate their collective energy field. In groups ruled by black holes and pirate patterns, most members don't feel safe to speak openly or make mistakes. The risk of a black hole being triggered is too high, so they keep quiet and give up, or hope that things will change. Groups unconsciously form black holes of stuck group energy by hiding and withholding energy and information that would lead to more productive results.

Just as individuals must release black hole emotions and other stuffed-away information to free their creative energy, so it is with groups. When any group is stuck in a pattern of withholding core information, they have curtailed their creative potential.

Many of us are more comfortable withholding information because it's familiar. Liz remembers the group pirating energy in her family. When she was four, she was standing on the back deck of their house, dressed up to have her picture taken. As she posed for the camera, her older sisters taunted her: "What an ugly little girl. What a stupid dress. Who would want a picture of her?" She remembers feeling humiliated, and buried the experience in a black hole. Now at age 48, she finds it easier to withdraw when challenged or dismissed in a group.

Energy pirating controls many groups. Often their members dread the group meetings and prefer to avoid them. When the output of a group is less productive than what the individuals could do on their own, the group is stuck. Honest core conversations that are open and inviting are scarce in groups dominated by pirating patterns.

One of the characteristics of a group stuck in pirate patterns is blame. Blame closes off free-flowing core communication. The following comments are examples of blame and indicate a stuck group in the workplace: "If it weren't for Joe, everything would be fine," "If Sally wouldn't talk all the time," "If Fred wasn't so domineering," or "If Karen would focus on her own job." Each of these comments protects the speakers' black holes with blame and maintains the established pirating patterns.

Stuck groups find someone or some group to fix with guilt. The denounced party can be a scapegoat, a subgroup, or another group. The marketing group may blame the sales department. Line workers may accuse management. Kids may impeach their parents. Countries make charges against other countries. The members of a stuck group are comforted by their agreement about whom to blame. The group comfort is thus maintained by separation. However, separation interrupts the flow of energy. As long as one group confers the blame on someone or another group, pirate patterns prevail. In the extreme, gang violence, racism, hate groups, and lynch mobs all connect through agreement about whom to blame. Even though group members are connected in righteous accusation, the flow of Source energy is severely limited.

Stuck groups typically exhibit two general patterns of behavior. One pattern is expressive aggressive behavior. Group members attack each other's ideas, put each other down, talk over each other, raise their voices to make a point, use foul language, or make personal attacks. Uneven participation, limited creativity, and a few people with high energy characterize these groups while others feel drained.

Another general pattern in stuck groups is avoidance and low participation. Most members have given up and no longer feel engaged or committed. Even when they think poor decisions are being made, they remain silent. Those who haven't completely given up may express their attitude by raising their eyebrows, or staring at the door, floor, or windows. The honest information that would put energy back into the group is shared elsewhere. At work, people talk about others in their cubicles, in the hallway, at the water cooler, in the rest rooms, or at home with their spouses—anywhere but at the group meetings.

These off-line meetings are simmering pots of mutual complaint. What happened in the group meeting is rehashed, wrongdoing is alleged, culprits are cited, frustrations are aired, and conclusions drawn. Rarely is anything done as a result of these informal lament sessions, but we usually feel better to have found agreement in our carping. Group energy in these off-line meetings is commonly higher than in the official group meetings because there is connection in agreement. But this is group energy pirating. It may feel good in the moment, but these groups are triggered by black holes that require continuous protection. Ultimately everyone who participates in pirating pays an energy price.

Sometimes off-line complaint sessions are more inclusive. Some of our favorite targets are management, government, corporations, Congress, Republicans, Democrats, environmentalists, the gas or electric company, the neighbors, family members, and the all-time, never-fail-favorite—the weather, especially in Oregon where everyone complains about the weather, "We know it's summer because the rain is warmer." People connect through mutual misery. There is more energy in commiseration than in isolation: we feel connected to our commiseration partner. We throw everything into a blame bag of complaint instead of becoming effective.

In this kind of group connection, if we stop complaining and take responsibility for our concerns, we break the group bond. Friends, fused in blame, may not know another way to connect. If we stop complaining, other members of the group may carp about us. If we stop participating in blame, we may temporarily lose the energy of commiseration. Many of us would prefer to be part of a group that is inviting, creative, and appreciative, but few of us know how to release and balance the energy of a stuck group.

Julie and I share the leadership of a group that meets regularly to study the work of Mary Morrissey, author of *Building Your Field of Dreams*. Zelda, a new group member, had been complaining about her daughter and blaming her ex-husband. Zelda's pattern was victim pirating. Several members had mentioned Zelda's behavior to me in private and one had dropped out of the group because of it. We had a stuck group. I spoke to Zelda about her participation, but her unconscious behavior hadn't changed.

One evening in the group after Zelda had begun complaining, Julie said, "I notice that I start feeling uncomfortable when you have been talking for a while." The room grew silent as everyone waited to see how Zelda would respond.

"Well, you're not uncomfortable when Joan goes on and on about her brother. Why does she get to take up time and I don't?" Zelda asked. "Joan speaks from her heart," Julie said. "I'm more comfortable with information that comes from your heart."

Zelda said that it was hard for her to speak from her heart because of the difficult problems she was facing. She said her brother was her only living relative besides her daughter, and her brother had cancer. She was terrified of losing him. As she spoke honestly from her core, her participation had a different effect on the group. The room became quiet. People were no longer fidgeting and looking at each other. All eyes were on Zelda. Julie was willing to be honest about her core and invited Zelda to a core interaction that freed the whole group to speak openly and honestly. Everyone left the meeting feeling the expansive energy of connection—synergy.

Few groups are willing to be this honest. People hide their core emotions and thoughts from each other, thereby creating a black hole in the group and making synergy impossible. By speaking our core truth, we may challenge group assumptions or norms. We may be attacked or discounted because we have confronted the established pirate patterns. Change, even to something better, can feel threatening. Others may not want to look at how they have contributed to what isn't working. In addition, we may not have enough practice speaking our core truth with love and acceptance, so our attempt to speak may become a pirate power play. Most of us are not skilled enough to be able to trump dominant pirate patterns. Challenging pirate patterns with core feelings seems risky, so most people don't speak up and share their core feelings and thoughts in a stuck group.

Consider what would happen if you decided to speak up. You might want to get a small group to back you. The time comes for you to say something. Perhaps a decision is pending that you care about, perhaps the boss is dominating the meeting, perhaps your project budget is being slashed, perhaps two people are arguing the merits of something irrelevant, and you choose this moment to share your core information. You begin with, "I think the communication in our group doesn't work very well. I would like our meetings to be more inviting and for everyone to feel free to participate." You turn to your allies for help, and they have disappeared into ceiling eyeballing and throat clearing. You are on your own. What's worse—you have just exposed your core to a pirating group. Experience that feeling for a moment. All eyes are trained on you. Someone responds, "What are you talking about? Do we have time for this? It's not on the agenda." Add notes from your own worst nightmare.

Now you must dig deep to find your core feelings and thoughts. You respond by saying. "I've been uncomfortable with how we interact for some time. I don't feel free to participate and I think we're losing momentum and energy. I believe that others feel that way too."

The response again might be, "What are you talking about?" Or someone might accept your invitation and agree with you. If so, you have dislodged the group. If others participate by offering their core feelings, thoughts, and wants, group energy is released. A group that can release stuck energy regularly generates creative energy and expands to a higher level of creativity. A connected group openly sharing core information explodes to synergy.

HOW TO EXPAND GROUP ENERGY

Risking honesty from your core experience is the natural path to synergy. Share your experience openly and claim what's true for you. Speak without blame about your personal frustrations or concerns, and ask for what you want. You can expect to be shot down according to the pirate pattern of the group. They may ignore you, attack you, humor you, or make fun of you. Accept whatever is said as normal behavior for a stuck group. What you do next is the crucial step. If you rejoin the group in silent blame or anguish, nothing changes. If you criticize the group, you invite blame. On the other hand, if you remain true to yourself and accept your new reaction, you can speak your new core experience. For example, you might say, "I'm feeling on the spot or uncomfortable, and I think there may be more options than we can see right now. I'd like to hear from others in our group who normally don't say much."

Remain true to yourself. Claim your frustrations, concerns, fears, desires, and longings. You have this perfect opportunity to be yourself steadfastly, tell your core truth, and invite others into core conversation. The pirates you have in your life are the perfect teachers for learning how to expand group energy. Learning this skill will earn you respect from others and respect from yourself. Notice how scary and good it feels to be vulnerable and create more expansive energy. Notice your relief and gratitude when someone steps in to join you. Let go of your need to prove anyone wrong for being the perfect teacher to lead you to yourself.

By speaking openly from your core experience and asking for what you want, you create safety for others to join you in core conversation. When one person joins, others will feel invited to a new level of conversation. This is not to suggest that interactions will be trouble free. Quite the contrary. Differing views will surface, conflicts will be discovered. Core conversation invites differing perspectives. Not everyone shares the same experience. Core conversations release group energy the way exploring black holes releases personal energy. With additional information available, energy and creative potential expand.

By initiating a core conversation, you may change the established pirate patterns of your group, and you may not. If you successfully initiate a core conversation, don't expect to stay there. Like mountain climbers, everyone in the party must become acclimated to the high-altitude camp. Everyone must be willing to participate in core conversations. This may take many trips from the base camp to the high-altitude camp. The base camp is a stuck group. Some people are never able to acclimate to high altitude. If they drag others back down the mountain into a stuck group, the group may never establish a high-altitude core conversation. If core conversations continue at high altitude, some may drop out. The movement from an expanded flowing balanced energy state back to a stuck group is quick and easy. Balanced energy is fluid and flows in and out of core conversations. A group stuck in pirate patterns doesn't flow easily to expanded levels of interaction.

The trek up the mountain from a stuck group expands the energy of the group, but there is a higher level of energy beyond the high-altitude camp. Expanded energy beyond what individuals alone can create is awesome, breathtaking, exhilarating. Synergy graces the top of the mountain. There are glaciers to climb and crevasses to cross before we reach the top, however.

Once we have invited others into core conversation, confusion and chaos may reign. Welcome these two indicators of energy flow. We are no longer stuck in the clarity of whom to blame. Chaos and confusion result when information is flowing and we haven't yet made sense of it. The mixing of new and confusing information may be unfamiliar and uncomfortable.

From this rich conversation, we can learn and create movement, new understanding, and more creative results. If we allow ourselves to stay connected and keep the dialogue open through the confusion, clarity will emerge—much like the game of Chinese checkers in which same-colored marbles are neatly aligned in triangles on a star-shaped game board. The object of the game is to move all our marbles across the game board to a new triangle. Players move their marbles across the middle of the game board to get to the other side (if the game goes well). As players move their marbles into the center of the game board, the central meeting space becomes a confusing mixture of colors and directions. Chaos is required before order is returned. Unless you move through the disorder (chaos) in the middle you cannot get to new ground.

Some work groups find synergy. People who have experienced

this expanded energy say that they love their work, they lose track of time because they are so absorbed in what they love, creative ideas flow, new opportunities appear, and they produce beyond what ordinary effort would suggest. People who are part of these work groups have fun working together and feel energized by their work.

Sometimes synergy flows when a crisis requires the focus of each member of the group. The emergency room at St. Charles Medical Center in Bend, Oregon, operates in an expanded energy state. When a patient arrives, people and resources flow into place to provide optimum care for that person. The night shift does this by "feel." There is a sense of what each patient needs and who will respond with care. Without many words, the team flows into action, each loving what he does. On the day shift, the process is different because the people are different. The daytime synergy flows from a plan for stations and responsibilities. Each member of the team helped decide on and develop the plan. All stations are ready at a moment's notice according to the plan. Each patient receives optimum care from the assigned staff and doctor. Once, a night shift nurse worked on the day shift. She felt awkward and uncertain because the approach was so different from that of the night shift. It's not the plan or the approach that creates synergy, it's the agreement and understanding of the people flowing together in what they do.

At the Innovative Learning Group, a consulting and training company in Eugene, Oregon, there is a celebration for family members at the end of each four-day personal development seminar. These seminars help people find their black holes and accept themselves at a core level. As people work together and help each other, the personal energy level of the group expands. At the celebration on Sunday night, when family and friends walk in and feel the expanded energy in the seminar room, many experience tears of joy. Children have an easier time adjusting to expansive energy than adults do. Adults aren't used to joyous, loving energy. I have watched little children's faces light up as they come into the celebration. Some adults have to leave the celebration before it is over because expanded love and acceptance can be overwhelming if you are not used to it.

When participants leave the seminar, they float on high energy for a week or so before noticing a return to a more normal energy level. For some, this descent back to normal energy is difficult. Once they've experienced expanded energy, they would like to remain in a joyous, accepting state. Outside the seminar, however, they are affected by the energy of larger groups. Most work groups and families are stuck groups. Few people are currently skilled in releasing their black holes and inviting others into core conversations, so synergy is unlikely to take the place of stuckness.

In creating synergy, the target skill is core conversation. Earlier in the book, I described core conversations as centered in your experience, aligned with your integrity, and unattached to the outcome. Core conversations sidestep all the pirating energy traps. Whether these conversations begin with fear and sadness or excitement and hope doesn't matter. Honesty energizes the conversation. Core conversations build the high-altitude camp from which expansive mountaintop experiences come.

When you talk about what is really going on in your group and endure the chaos and confusion of new ground, a sense of direction emerges. You may not notice the change in group energy in a core conversation, but you will notice the energy of synergy. The change in energy is like an electron changing its state. As an electron orbits an atom, it can disappear from a lower level and appear in a higher level simultaneously. Scientists say the electron pops to a new valence shell, or leaps to a more expanded energy level. Synergy in a group works the same way. Energy expands instantly. The conditions are core honesty, acceptance, and agreement. The skills we need to meet these conditions are acknowledgment, core conversation, and surrendering the outcome. Synergy is the gift. If you practice these skills, one day you will notice its presence—a sense of joy, fun, excitement, love, flow, productivity, timelessness, connection, camaraderie, and expansive energy.

After my mother died, my two brothers, my sister, and I gathered to talk about her memorial service. My dad had asked each of us to speak at the service. The last few weeks had united us as we spent many hours together, talking, praying, and crying. Now, despite our grieving, we needed a plan. We assumed that the oldest, John, would speak first at the service, and that the rest of us would follow in our birth order—Jesse, Bill, and Helen. But Helen had the courage to say that she didn't want to speak last.

"I'm afraid if I go last, everything I want to say will have been said, and I'll stand there weeping and nothing will come out," said Helen. "Would you rather go first? We could reverse the order and I'll go last," John offered.

"My heart hurts so much I can't even think straight. I guess I'd like to be tucked in the middle, so if I get up there and flounder, someone will rescue me," Helen replied.

"I feel the same way," said Bill. "I'm comfortable with large audiences, but I don't know whether I'll be able to walk up there, let alone say something. Maybe I could read some of her poetry."

"I'm scared too," I said. "But if I can, I'd like to talk about these last few weeks we've had together because of how Mom died with such dignity." The lump in my throat stopped me from saying more.

"I think the only way I'll be able to say anything is if I show slides," said John. "I think I could talk about the pictures. I have some wonderful slides of Mom when we were younger."

"I think John should go first with the slide show," said Bill.

"And Jesse, you should go last because you're talking about the end of her life," said Helen.

"Then Helen and Bill could be in the middle," I added.

With the grace of a poignant moment, we created family synergy. The next day, over 200 people experienced our love and support. Afterward, at least a dozen people told us that it was the most meaningful service they had ever attended. Our willingness to be honest and connected grew into a beautiful tribute to our mother.

Once you have taken the risk to speak from your heart, the potential for change is present. Others notice because core honesty is unusual. There are no pirating barbs, no blame arrows. Your words are clean and inviting. Will others know how to respond? At first they may not. They may continue to play pirate games. A stuck group may resist your invitation. As you continue to offer your core perspective, however, others learn from you and without realizing it begin to speak more honestly. Your open expanded energy attracts Source energy. Core conversations are inviting. My sister Helen invited us to a core conversation by honestly sharing core information, even though it challenged our assumptions. Her courage opened the door to synergy.

ENERGY PRINCIPLES FOR GROUP INTERACTION

I believe there are four fundamental physical energy principles that apply to human energy fields and energy pirating. I developed these principles by relating some of the laws of the physical universe to human experience.

These principles govern both individual energy fields and group energy fields. Whenever people touch us, emotionally, intellectually, physically, or spiritually, they become a part of our field. As we work with others our fields merge. If our energy is aligned emotionally and intentionally our work is easier and more energized. If we react to people they affect our energy field. All these effects merge our energy fields with others. The more open we are with another person, the more energized our merged field. The more distant we are either physically or emotionally, the less energized our joint field. However, it is not possible to separate our energy fields completely from the people we work with, talk to, live with, befriend or resist. Whether our experience of others in a merged field is open and accepting or distant and rejecting, our fields influence each other.

These principles govern our interactions and relationships across a whole spectrum of human experience, including both small groups of two up to congregations, including groups enjoying creative, expansive energy and groups locked in pirating patterns.

What we energize expands.

As we direct our creative energy—our thoughts, beliefs, emotions, and actions—we focus our energy, like a magnifying glass concentrates the sun's energy on one point. If we focus on problems, we will see more problems. If we put our energy into solutions, we expand the pool of possible solutions. If we search for black holes, we will become aware of our black holes. If we look for pirates, we'll encounter pirates. We energize the focus of our attention.

Our thoughts, emotions, and beliefs commonly become our reality. If we believe that we are likable, we will behave in ways that people like. If we believe that we are not attractive, we will feel unattractive and act that way. If we yearn for something, we experience yearning instead of getting what we want. If we feel grateful for what we have, what we have expands.

Typically, what we give out comes back to us in one form or another. This is not a one-to-one correlation, nor do we necessarily receive in kind from the same person we gave to; but generally, if we are kind to people, people will be good to us. If we blame people, they are likely to blame us. If we pirate energy, we are likely to experience energy pirating in response. If we are loving and extend our good will, others are likely to respond with love and good will toward us. What we consciously put energy into and what our black holes attract may be different. However it is the cumulative effect of our conscious focus and our black holes that determines our total energy field and, therefore, what shows up in our lives.

Our interactions are governed more by the nature of the energy field than by our individual nature.

The black holes and pirate patterns in human energy fields determine the patterns of our interactions. Each of us is capable of a broad range of behavior. In one group, our actions are completely different from what we do in another. It depends on which black holes we are avoiding and who is pirating from whom. Once we react to mask a black hole, a pattern is formed in the field. Which black hole is triggered depends on our own black holes and the pirate patterns in the group field. Out of an infinite variety of possible reactions, what shows up in our behavior is dependent on the established patterns in the group field. Once patterns of interaction are established between people, the person engaged in energy pirating can trigger the same black hole easily and repeatedly. This is why couples tend to have the same disagreement over and over.

Unless we release our black holes, and consciously choose to act differently, pirate patterns and black holes will have the greatest influence on our reactions. Once established, pirate patterns will continue because the individuals are locked in a relationship governed by the field.

We train others to react to us.

We adopt patterns of behavior that avoid our black holes, although we are usually unaware that we do this. Others will notice our patterns and react to us. Our actions and reactions establish regular patterns of interaction that train others how to treat us. Again, we tend to be unaware that we are training others.

For example, if someone says hello and we don't respond, we are training him not to say hello or continue the conversation. If we show our appreciation to someone, we are training him to do more of what we appreciate. If we believe that we are unlovable, people using pirate strategies learn that they can get what they want from us by threatening to withdraw their love. Our reactions train them.

On the other hand, if someone pirating energy suggests that we are a problem and we have already released our black holes and changed our beliefs, we know the pirate's suggestion is probably not true. We know that we have done the best we can. We can then be open to learn from whatever is said and help this person with his concerns. If we are curious instead of reactive, we train people to approach us differently.

Someone unconsciously using pirate patterns can be retrained and regular patterns of interaction changed. These patterns can be changed quickly. Not all patterns are as responsive, but if we release our black holes, our own patterns change and our interactions are so different that it seems as if other people have changed. Changing the pirating patterns in your groups requires that you release you own black holes and react in a new way. When you choose a new response, pirate patterns liquefy in preparation for change. What happens next depends on how ready you are for a new pattern.

Energy flows though the path of least resistance.

If we have a black hole that is easy to trigger, someone pirating energy will find it. If we release our black holes, the patterns in our personal energy field shift, which also affects our group energy fields. Each person in the group energy field has a stake in maintaining the current patterns, because if we don't react and give the person who is pirating energy what he wants, someone else will be the focus of the next pirate attack. No one wants the job of supporting energy pirating. As long as we are willing to remain the victim of the group's pirate pattern, others are relieved of the job. If we physically leave a group energy field by quitting our job or breaking off contact with family members, the patterns of the group adjust. Someone else is given the job of reacting to the pirate patterns. If we join another energy field without releasing our black holes, there will be people in the new group who use pirate strategies that trigger our black holes.

Unfortunately, the same is true if you are energy pirating. The patterns set in motion in the group energy field are hard to change. You may find yourself engaging in behavior you do not like in yourself—energy pirating behavior that you seem unable to stop.

Fortunately, human energy fields are different from most electromagnetic fields in that we can make conscious choices to change them. The way to transform pirating relationships is to alter our own reactions. We can change our behavior by releasing our black holes and thus transform the beliefs and intentions that drive our reactions. If we remain steadfast in a new behavior, we can transcend the behavior patterns of our group energy fields. Leaving an energy field does not change our vulnerability to energy pirating, because pirating works as long as we have black holes. If we choose to release our black holes and act differently, the patterns in our energy fields adapt. People who previously pirated energy from us, find other sources of energy, and new patterns are established.

We affect all people in every group we are any part of, and they impact us. We train others how to treat us and they train us. As we play our part, energy weaves our interactions together in a pattern. When we are open to Source energy and speak from our hearts our energy resonates in the core of others and awakens a desire to connect. Most people are not aware of awakening, but they will naturally choose to move closer to us or further away.

If two or more group members regularly converse honestly with heartfelt openness, the norms of the group rise to a new level of candor, connection, and honesty. The group adjusts and includes all members in the search for direction and flow. Flow is determined by the willingness of the group to let go of outcomes, be open to learning, stay connected, and take accountability for their own black holes. The more ownership of black holes and the less pirating of energy, the safer the group will be. The safer the group, the more people will open to the flow.

Those who are unwilling to move beyond the protection of pirating will gravitate away from a group that is developing through core conversation. Most will join, but some are not ready. We must respect their need to remain protected for a while longer. One person can open the flow of a group by being willing to speak without blame. One person, willing to be honest and vulnerable, can create the capacity for patterns to become liquid.

We risk producing miracles with synergy. And we risk the loss of relationships that aren't ready for new patterns. If we no longer want relationships built on pirate patterns, it is a risk worth taking. Groups that have found agreement and developed a vision of what they want are a powerful force. If one member of a group is doubting or scared, other group members can hold the vision. Every member of a group will waver or feel afraid from time to time. The whole doesn't suffer as long as honest concerns can be expressed and released within the group. Yet the natural tendency in groups when things are going well is to stop core conversations. The fear is that if we doubt or question what is already good, we may lose our creative energy. Just the opposite is true. The power of a group is lost only when honest expressions are withheld. Any withholding separates the group energy and dismantles synergy.

Groups functioning in truth and acceptance release powerful creative synergy. Two or more individuals joining together in synergy can shed light on the shadows of their lives. Every one of us is capable of creating powerful expansive synergy in every interaction and area of our lives.

When we release our black holes, clear the air with core conversations, and guide and move our energy with intent, we open to the flow of life force energy. We can clear a path for Source energy by keeping our agreements, aligning our internal experiences with our words and actions, observing and accepting our experiences in meditation, and renewing our energy in nature. These practices to balance and align our energy require discipline, patience, and trust. All of us who are willing to start again when we fall short, and accept that we are in the perfect place to begin anew, will feel the flow of Source energy.

Chapter Nine

Leaving an Energy Legacy

....

My friend Dirk and I stood in line at an airlines counter at the Portland Airport. The line stretched across the lobby and snaked through four rows of people confined in the velvet-roped pathway. Six agents worked the counter. After twenty minutes I remarked to the man in front of us that the line wasn't moving. He said he had been in the line for 45 minutes and hadn't seen any movement either. Another man two rows in front of us added that he had been in line for two-and-a-half hours and hadn't gotten anywhere. Someone else chimed in that some of the airline's pilots were on strike and that several flights had been canceled. He added that all the flights that were still scheduled were overbooked.

Dirk looked at me and suggested we go back to curbside to check our bags and then go directly to the gate. Ten minutes later at the gate when Dirk turned to get our tickets out, his elbow knocked the cup of hot tea out of my hands. The tea spilled down the front of my sweater and onto the floor. I said, "Whoops, that will teach me not to stand too close." We laughed and the gate agent smiled.

I dabbed up the tea, and we waited for our seat assignments. The agent reported that every seat on the plane was taken and there were no adjoining seats left. "Oh, well," I said. "How about exit-row, middle seats, got any of those?" She assigned us two exit-row, middle seats, tucked our boarding passes under her keyboard, and said she'd try to seat us together. I realized I was completely happy, and if Dirk and I weren't able to sit together, it wouldn't affect my mood. I was open to whatever was going to happen. At the last minute, we got our new boarding passes for seats 17c and d—an aisle and a middle seat together. We thanked the agent and boarded the plane.

As we settled into the only unoccupied seats on the plane, the people around us were grumbling about the long delays and bad seating assignments. No one seemed very happy, except us. I felt grateful and balanced. Forty minutes into our flight, the flight attendants served us lasagna for dinner. I was starving, but since I don't eat butter or cheese, I asked the stewardess if there were any special meals left over. She said she'd check and soon returned with curried vegetables. I marveled that there was an extra vegan dinner on the plane. That had never happened to me before, and the meal was delicious.

When we touched down in Denver, we had an hour-and-a-half before our connecting flight. We walked down the concourse to a bar and grill. The Colorado hockey playoffs were on television and the room was packed with people to see the game. Passengers and luggage were scattered everywhere in the dimly lit bar, but there was one table in the middle that had a light directly over it. It was perfect. We ordered Fat Tire Ale. Now, if you're ever in the Denver airport and you like beer, I highly recommend Fat Tire Ale— unbelievably smooth and Friday night quenching. We realized that we were in some kind of zone. Everything seemed effortless. The pool of light around us seemed to get bigger as we talked and laughed, and included the waitress and other passengers in our banter.

On our connecting flight we had the exit row to ourselves, with room to stretch out comfortably. As the plane took off, we watched the jeweled lights of Denver spread out below us and a clear white full moon emerge from a layer of clouds on the horizon, a breathtaking sight. A single shaft of moonlight beamed down below the cloud layer, following us in our flight. When we came close to our destination, the moon reflected off the Rio Grande like a silver snake leading us into Albuquerque.

I tell this story because we were participating in creating an energy legacy. My inner joy matched the experiences we found on our journey, and what we wanted appeared effortlessly. This kind of joy is contagious. Even when we don't interact with others, we contribute to a collective energy field that affects everyone. I don't think there is an explanation for this phenomenon. But I believe that releasing black holes, changing pirating patterns, and aligning our energy with Source allows us to pop magically into an expansive flow that is who we are at our best.

It isn't only big events that are fulfilling, though it would be great to have all our work and relationship interests satisfied. It's the small moments, like the silver moonlight and the perfect table for two, that feed our joy. But these moments are the result of our internal state. Some of us look to outside events—a new car, a promotion, the perfect relationship—to make us happy. I think it works the other way around. When we are filled with joy, when we anticipate the next moment with a sense of wonder, the situation will match our internal creative energy.

The flow of Source energy is entirely ours to guide, and we determine whether we experience it as expansive or constricted. Source is energy flowing through us. I have shared some of the ways to enhance and expand our capacity to draw Source energy through our energy fields. Wherever you are on your path opening to the Source, it is up to you to decide how to wield the energy that flows though your field.

In every moment, our energy fields flow with mental, emotional, physical, and spiritual energy. Sometimes we color our energy with love and joy. At other times, we flavor it with critical judgments. We can reach out with acceptance or disengage with rejection. Inclusive, connecting energy expands our collective life force, while the disconnection of blame and judgment diminishes our collective life force.

All creative energy is Source energy. Our formative information is fueled by Source. We are the regulators of creative Source energy that flows through us. Source itself is neutral in that it supports whatever we choose. We consciously and unconsciously wield Source energy. Source fuels our joyous energy when we consciously choose joy. Source also fuels our fearful energy when we are afraid.

Whether Source flows openly, freely, and consciously, or is constricted in black holes, it is still Source energy. We are the ones who wield and choose how to direct it. Our choices include hate, anger, and fear, as well as joy, love, and acceptance. Like electricity, Source energy can be used for good or ill. We become the stewards of this resource, and how we choose to use Source energy creates value or causes harm. We can reach out to include and accept others, or exclude them with blame and anger. Source accepts and supports our free will.

We value electricity because it lights our evenings and early mornings. We appreciate the energy that cooks our food and runs our televisions. We enjoy our computers and electronic equipment. Electricity doesn't value one use over another. If we plug in worn insulation or faulty appliances, we may start a fire. The electricity doesn't stop flowing to keep us from harm. Joy and fear are equally powerful. If we intend harm, which is fueled by fear, electric shock can be a lethal weapon. Electricity is there to assist us with our choices. Source energy also assists us with our choices. If we keep some of our emotional memories in black holes, these black holes unconsciously misdirect, filter, and constrict Source energy. Constricted Source energy creates our unconscious black hole fears and limiting beliefs.

How we use Source is similar to how we use electricity. We can include others, accepting their strengths and weaknesses, or we can judge them and criticize them. Source energy assists us with this choice. We can choose to create more love or more fear. Whatever we choose is acceptable to the all-inclusive, all-accepting Source. However, the free flow of Source energy is available only when our energy is flowing freely. Source energy unconsciously constricted by black holes tends to snare difficulties. Constricted energy can't surge around obstacles. Free will is one of the laws of life on Earth. We have the awesome responsibility to choose how we wield or constrict our life force energy.

In making our choices, we can be guided by the first fundamental principle of energy field theory. What we energize expands. Another way to phrase this principle is that what we do to and for others expands to include us. In other words, our life force energy has a boomerang effect. This is similar to the Hindu and Buddhist principle of karma.

Karma is defined by the *American Heritage Dictionary* as "the sum and consequences of a person's actions during successive phases of his existence." In the United States, karma is commonly used to explain cause and effect. When something unfortunate happens, someone may say, "Bad karma." When something good happens, someone may say, "What goes around comes around." The idea is that someone had it coming, good fortune or bad. Many people believe that if they harm others, karma will bring similar harm to them or someone they love. The common view of karma in America is a misunderstanding of the principle. Karma is not action and retribution, but an energy principle. Source energy is balanced in perfect love. Human energy comes into balance over time by reflecting back to us how we are not in balance with perfect love. If our thoughts and actions are not aligned with love, we will experience the effects of an unbalanced system. Even if we give to others, we may not be fully accepting of ourselves. The imbalance will show up as an opportunity to learn to be more accepting. If we accept ourselves but judge others, if we direct but are not in balance with Source energies—the wider the gap is between our creative energy (our emotions, beliefs, intentions, and perfectly balanced Source energy) and the greater the disturbance in our energy fields. Our actions can create even more imbalance. The purpose of this imbalance is greater consciousness. As we create disturbances in our energy fields, we encounter difficulties and challenges. These challenges support learning. If we stuff these disasters and tragedies into our black holes, we lose the opportunity to learn. If we lose our opportunities to learn, we create more challenges. The more we constrict our consciousness with black holes, the more we experience human tragedy.

Source energy is nonjudgmental. Human events are generated by imbalance, similar to weather systems that tend to flow toward balance. High pressure areas flow toward low pressure. Wind and storms are created by imbalance in the system. The greater the imbalance, the more severe the storm can be. Energy systems also flow toward balance. Personal energy, like physical energy, can change form, but it cannot be destroyed. Just as positively charged lightning is attracted by negative ground forces to balance physical energy systems, so, too, human energy systems flow toward balance. And perfect balance is perfect love.

Thoughts, intentions, emotions, and actions are all energy generators. Think about things that have happened in your life. Have you initiated imbalance in the system? The more I am aware of my intentions, emotions, thoughts, and actions, the more I am aware of subtle ways I have created imbalance. Notice the effect your energy has on your life and the lives of those around you.

I caution you not to explain what happens to you or your loved ones as karma. I believe that karma is only one of many forces at work in our energy fields. Everyone's intentional, mental, and emotional energy drives the forces of the universe. Each person on Earth flavors and directs Source energy. The effect of greater balance is a change in human consciousness. A growing awareness to choose our thoughts, feelings, and intentions consciously contributes to more or less balance or imbalance. Our energy affects our communities. Some groups direct their energy to cleaning up neighborhoods, supporting schools, and collecting contributions for the less fortunate. These groups are creating community energy legacies. Other groups create separation through benign neglect, prejudice, or elegant gated developments that separate people and energy. Communities and larger groups direct and create fields of energy. Together we influence national and world energy systems. National energy fields may affect us with disturbances such as war or the outpouring of relief for disasters. Though we may not have initiated these experiences, how we react to them determines our energy contribution to the whole.

I believe that our human energy system is an impressive weave of energy threads flowing and moving into balance. Each thought, action, and feeling contributes to the balance or imbalance of the whole. Just as the tide comes in and goes out, just as the sun rises and sets, energy systems also have cycles. I believe there are global cycles of expansive caring energy balanced by life-depleting cycles of drought, starvation, and war. Life is a mixture of delightful as well as challenging times, pleasurable and difficult experiences. The natural ebb and flow has a purpose. Black holes are easier to find in painful situations. Perhaps the world community also has black holes of hidden pain and blind spots. Community and global disasters can bring us together to release the lack of caring and the isolation.

We don't have ultimate control, but we do significantly influence what shows up in our lives. We choose how we react to circumstances. We choose whether we see the dark cloud or the silver lining. We choose whether to laugh about the hot tea spilled on us, or to grumble about it. We choose our intentions, and they then become the creative force in our lives. We contribute mental, emotional, physical, and spiritual energy in every moment. We choose whether to open our lives to a more expansive flow of Source. We are responsible for the creation of our reactions, our influence, our beliefs, and our choices.

Our thoughts and actions affect ourselves as well as others. If we think unkind thoughts about ourselves, we affect the whole just as strongly as if we had criticized someone else. If we hurt ourselves, we hurt the whole. We are all a part of Source. We deserve to be loved, honored, and respected. We can choose to do that for ourselves.

Choosing a loving energy legacy is about being true to ourselves. It's about integrity, doing what we say we will do, being true to our emotions, and telling the difficult core truth with love. It's about understanding and respecting the balance of the universal energy system. Our personal responsibility is to release our black holes so that we do not act compulsively in ways that do not serve us or others. As we love, we draw more loving energy to us, just as when we whisper, others tend to whisper back. As we accept others and allow expansive loving energy to return to us, we are developing a new, more balanced pattern. We attract what we are becoming.

I think we have much more to learn about the subtleties of balance. This morning, at my house on the Oregon coast, I was curled up in a blanket, cozy, warm, and safe in the company of dear friends. We were talking about local and national political issues. Each person had an opinion about each of these issues, and no two people thought exactly alike. I was struck by how exceptional this open conversation was, in which we honored our subtle differences. Thinking about our fast-paced, electronically supported lives, I wondered if in the developed world we are losing our ability to honor perspectives that are different from our own. I would like to think that we are increasing our awareness through conversations that challenge our thinking and trigger our feelings and beliefs.

But I worry that such conversations are rare. What we lose is multi-dimensional creative energy that launches groups to new levels of awareness and understanding. Creating this kind of shared understanding requires that we handle our own black holes when they are triggered. It requires that we tell the core truth about our personal experiences. It requires that we hold a space for other perspectives that challenge and even threaten what we see as sound and right. It requires an accountability that goes far beyond doing what we say we will do—an accountability that says, "I respect you. I am open to your thoughts and experience. I can handle how it affects me. I can admit when one of my black holes is triggered and I can deal with it. I can surrender to my own process and not blame you. I don't have to change your thinking to relieve myself of feeling threatened. I can allow tightness in my gut to signal that I might be wrong, and yet I can still value you, despite my uncomfortable feelings."

Each of us sees and understands only a small slice of the whole. In order to broaden our understanding we must explore perspectives that we don't share. We can invite multiple perspectives at work and with neighbors and friends. We can warmly welcome diametrically opposed views. We can embrace the perspectives of other cultures and other ethnic and religious groups.

Our willingness to be in this soup of opinions, experiences, and perspectives rests on our ability to handle our own reactions. If we have this ability, we can join this rich mixture without projecting blame or judging others, without sinking into guilt and shame.

Though it is sometimes hard to admit, we are each fallible and we are each having the perfect experience at any given moment from which to learn and choose more wisely.

——————— · · · · · ———————

My friend Susan openly shares her joyful energy wherever she goes. She is working on releasing her black holes and giving up her pirating patterns. Susan's balanced, loving energy overflows. One day, I went with her to the grocery store and listened to her conversation with the checkout clerk.

"I probably couldn't find the mustard if you put it on the checkout stand with a neon sign over it, but one of your clerks was so helpful, I found everything I came for and much more. I probably shouldn't come shopping when I'm so hungry, but I'll eat it all eventually. How has your day been?" The clerk smiled. "It's been a long day, but I'm nearly at the end of my shift."

"I'll bet you're tired of being on your feet all day. I hope you can pamper yourself tonight," Susan said. "No, not with my grandkids at home."

"Grandkids! I can't wait until I have grandchildren some day. How many do you have?" Susan asked. The clerk grinned, "I've got three of the cutest granddaughters."

When Susan left the store, the clerk was still grinning. Susan's joyful energy probably expanded and made his little girls happier that evening. Susan's interaction was self-energizing too. When she finished shopping, she had more energy than when she began. Her energy invites loving, accepting energy back to her. She starts the flow and is filled by the return. Susan can give away her expansive energy, but she is not depleted. As long as she is true to herself and does what she really wants to do, the more she gives, the more it flows back to her.

I try to live like Susan. Sometimes I succeed, sometimes I fail. One evening I drove home from Eugene to Portland after a day of sailing on Fern Ridge Reservoir. It was after 10 p.m. by the time I reached the outskirts of Portland, and I was fighting to stay awake. I turned up Carmen Drive and slowed at the empty cross street. As

I turned uphill a half block from my townhouse, red and blue police lights flashed behind me. I turned into my driveway and stepped out of my car with the police car lights flashing right behind me.

"I am so glad to be home," I said to the policeman who approached me. "I've been sailing all day in Eugene and I wasn't sure I could stay awake for the drive home."

I could see that this kind of threw him. "You know you didn't come to a complete stop at the stop sign on the corner of Carmen and Parkview, and you only slowed down for the next stop sign. It's a danger to other cars on the road to glide through stop signs like that."

I agreed with him. "You're right. I didn't make a very complete stop. I was just so glad to be almost home. I couldn't wait to get out of the car and be off the road." His voice softened. "I understand. You were almost home. Those were the last two stop signs on a long trip. You probably shouldn't be driving when you're so tired. So go get some rest and be more careful when you come to a stop sign." "You're not going to give me a ticket?" I said.

"No, I'm just glad you're home safely." I thanked him and waved as he left the driveway.

The officer's energy shift was visible—my openness and acceptance had jolted him. My intention was to be my loving, truthful self. When my intention is to interact with as much love and truth as is possible for me, I am usually amazed by what happens.

——— • • • • • ———

When we think of legacy, we think in terms of programs, buildings, inheritance, history, and the remembrance of friends and family. While all of these may be valuable, they have the same impermanence as human existence. Programs change, buildings are demolished, inheritance is spent, history is rewritten, and our friends and family eventually leave their own legacies. We ceaselessly rebuild our material world. Change is the one constant.

However, each of us leaves a lasting legacy of energy. We exude a field of mental and emotional energy every moment of our lives. This field of energy contributes to the system of energy that is life, a contribution that is lasting because energy cannot be destroyed. We always have the opportunity to transform human energy into more expansive loving energy—we humans are transformers of energy. We eat plants and animals to convert chemical energy into thinking, feeling, and action energy. We allow Source to flow through us to create our dreams in the material world. We can increase the flow of expansive joyous energy, or we can expand fearful energy through pirating. We can generate hostility in groups by feeling hostile. We can generate love with understanding. Our silent emotions influence others. We have a choice in every moment about how we contribute.

Leaving an energy legacy is like growing a garden. If we plant flowering shrubs and trees, everyone who visits our garden will experience the beauty of what we have planted. If we neglect our garden and it becomes a tangle of thorns, then others may be scratched by what we are growing. If we spray our garden with poisons, others may be harmed. Our energy legacy can be experienced in the same way. Wherever we love, a trace of joyful energy remains. Wherever we are angry, a trace of anger remains. When we are dishonest, jealous, cruel, or hateful, others react and manifest more of this fear-based energy. When we are truthful, loving, kind, joyous, and openhearted, others reflect this energy and more joyful energy is created.

These energy legacies are palpable and can be experienced in many holy places. We can sense the reverence and expansive energy of these. Some churches, cathedrals, music halls, ancient forests, and other holy gathering places exude expansive loving energy. When we are open to the stillness there, we can feel a sense of peace in our own energy. They are the energy legacies from past generations.

Similarly, there are places filled with disturbing energy. The gas chambers of Auschwitz still hold the agony and suffering of thousands, leaving a legacy of anguish that visitors can feel within the walls. I visited a native Heida tribal village in the Queen Charlotte Islands of British Columbia. It was the site of hundreds of deaths from smallpox after white traders gave infected blankets to the natives. The trees and rocks of the burial ground seemed draped with a sorrow that I felt as I walked through the abandoned village.

Energy legacies come not only from the past. I recently stopped at a gas station in a small town on my way to the Oregon coast. It's illegal to pump your own gas in Oregon. I waited five minutes while an attendant stood staring at the ground, his shoulders slumped. I got out of my car and waited to see what would happen. After a few minutes, he turned and slowly walked toward my car. "Whadya want?" "Fill it up with regular," I said.

He turned to fumble with the gas pump. I walked to the door of the mini-market and as soon as I was inside, my energy contracted as though I needed to protect myself. I asked the woman at the cash register where the rest rooms were. She looked at me for a moment without answering. "Outside," she said. "Outside around the corner?" I said pointing left. "Outside," she repeated.

Glad to step back into the fresh air, I opened the rest room door and noticed that cleaning was not a priority. I completed my transaction for gasoline and commented about the beautiful weather. The clerk handed me my change and never looked up.

As I drove out of the station, I thought about the energy of place. There are places where people have narrowed their interactions to pirating patterns and live in fear of each other. These places can be found anywhere people gather, neighborhoods, bars, restaurants. These legacies affect every person who travels through those spaces. These are lasting energy legacies because they unconsciously influence others to perpetuate them. They can only be changed with sufficient conscious loving attention.

We are each creating an energy legacy right now. Are we open to the truth of our experience and holding our reactions gently, or are we denying our feelings and withholding our energy, or are we blasting others with our reactions? We can choose how to respond in each moment. We can pirate energy in order to feel more energized, or we can open to the flow of Source. Whatever we choose, we create a legacy.

Your legacy is your contribution to the human energy continuum. What are you contributing? Will your energy support creative solutions in future generations, or will you leave pirate energy to be transformed by others? Energy is the legacy we leave. Energy is the legacy we inherit. We are the transformers.

The energy legacy we leave affects the level of creativity with which future generations meet political and environmental challenges. We have everything to gain from allowing Source to flow through us. We have everything to gain from recognizing our false beliefs and accepting the truth about ourselves. Our bodies are far more than carbon digesters. With a physical body, we have the power to transform troubling, scary experiences into love and joy. We have the emotional capacity to expand our energy to warm the hearts of hardened pirates. We have the creative capacity to expand the flow of Source that is the suchness of life. We have the cellular structure to guide the creative forces of the Universe.

Our challenge does not lie in facing others; it is in facing our own fears, our own history—ourselves. If we are courageous on this new frontier, we leave an energy legacy of love and joy.

If you have been given an especially tough life assignment—childhood abuse, surviving the holocaust, the loss of a child—you are probably a special soul whose work here is to shift the clouds of humiliation, pain, and loss into the clear light of love through forgiveness and acceptance. There may be no more important work on Earth. Each one of us has the capacity to transform personal trauma into peaceful acceptance.

Communities, countries, and institutions can't transform hatred into love. Only human beings have that capacity, lying within each one of us. It lies in our ability to release our black holes. We are not alone in the black hole experience; other people have similar reactions and feel similar feelings when they are triggered. All of us feel less than capable sometimes. We feel unloved sometimes. We feel that we just can't deal with our lives sometimes. We don't always trust our ability to create what we want. We share many of the same human weaknesses. If each of us were to transform our own reactions, our world would be transformed. Changing our own reactions to life's tragedies makes it easier to help others facing similar circumstances. This is the work of our souls.

Our work is before us each day. We don't need to look next door to find the problem with our neighborhood. We don't need to look across national borders to find the trouble plaguing our planet. We don't need to travel the globe to find a way to serve. Each one of us is right where we're needed to transform our world. When Lady Di asked Mother Theresa where her help was most needed, Mother Teresa responded, "If you had been asked to live in the streets of Calcutta, then that would be your work. But, you have been asked to be the Princess of Wales and that is where your work is." Expansive energy does not flow from denying our own needs while taking care of others. Expansive energy flows from self-acceptance, self-love, keeping our agreements, and thinking, feeling, and doing what we say we will do.

It's not a question of whether or not we contribute. We do, whether we intend to or not. Every human action, emotion, and thought contribute to the balance of our human energy system. What we energize expands. Black holes create black hole reactions. I can't complete a successful journey by believing that I will fail. Our conscious and unconscious energy draws to us the physical manifestation of our beliefs, emotions, and intentions. I can't build a fulfilling life by constricting Source energy. We influence each moment of our lives by how we live and the energy legacy we leave. We each add one thread to the tapestry of life. Will your thread add a fuller, brighter, more alive color to the design?

I believe that together we can experience a more balanced and loving collective energy field. I have had glimpses of this expanded level, and these experiences have given me hope that we are evolving and can get there. The irony is that unless I love and accept my current level of awareness and the whole of humanity as it is, I cannot expand beyond my limitations. My love and acceptance must start where I am. I can only trust the truth of my own experience. Grounded and centered in my core awareness, I touch others with my joy and my sadness. In this place I understand and acknowledge that others are in the perfect place for them to be today.

I can hold a vision and commit to doing my part to advance this vision, enrolling and enlisting those who share it. The more I work with you, the more we empower our shared intentions. I can help create synergy by finding common ground with you, connecting with you, sharing my core experience with you, and accepting yours. When I feel lost, alone, angry, scared, or sad, I can accept that I am in the perfect place for me to be. I can allow my core emotions to move, change, and flow with acceptance. I can act on the nudges that reveal my part in creating our shared intentions. I can notice when my energy feels expansive and accept it when it contracts. I can ask for the experience of balanced energy and accept what comes.

I invite you to:

- Become familiar with your black holes.
- Be aware of when you are pirating energy.
- Explore and release your black holes.
- Share your core experience.
- Reflect the core experience of others.
- Align your life with source energy.
- Meditate to strengthen your soul.
- Visit wild, natural places for inspiration.
- Connect with others to create synergy.
- Appreciate that everything you think, feel, and do leaves an energy legacy.

Appendices

....

ENERGY FIELD EXERCISE

This is an exercise you can do to become more aware of energy fields. Find a friend who would like to explore energy fields with you. Face each other, knees nearly touching. Choose one person to create the energy field, the other to be the receiver and observer. If you are the person observing the field, notice what is created without judgment. Remain open and sense the emotions that are generated by your partner.

If you are the one to create the energy field and want it to be loving and expansive, look at your partner with love and admiration. Think about what this friend has meant to you. Notice the little things about this person that you adore or admire. Don't say anything, just think of how much you appreciate this friendship. Let your energy flow toward your friend with no reservations. After a couple of minutes, shift back to normal, and talk about how the energy field felt to each of you.

For a fearful, separating field, think of a frustrating situation that has happened to you or someone you care about. Picture the person you feel is responsible for the situation. Mentally paste this person's face over your friend's face. Feel your frustration and anger radiating outward as you blame the person in the mask for what has happened. Once you have created this energy, continue for only ten seconds. This kind of energy is so powerful, it can be damaging even as an exercise. Immediately let go of blame. Talk about how the energy field felt to each of you. If you have any difficulty detecting differences in the energy field, don't worry. The perception of energy fields can take time to develop. Generating the field will give you a better sense of what is created.

Now switch roles. If you had the creative role before, notice the difference. Talk about what you discover. What was different in the two fields? What reaction did you have? Did you sense your reaction in a specific part of your body—your head, your chest, your belly? By noticing our physical sensations, we can locate our emotions and release them. Use this exercise to develop your physical awareness. Talk with your friend about your experience.

BLACK HOLE RELEASE QUESTIONS

Every situation is different. Ask your friends to use these questions for guidance, and to trust their own thinking to help you explore your black hole.

Mind-Centered Release Questions

Claiming your black hole:

- Are you in a black hole?
- What are you experiencing?
- What are you noticing?
- Where are you feeling a reaction in your body?
- What does it feel like?

Exploring past connections:

- When did you feel this way before?
- What is your earliest memory of feeling this way?
- What is happening?
- How old are you?
- Where are you?
- Who else is there?
- What are you doing?

- What do you see?
- What do you hear people saying?
- How are you feeling?

Expanding the experience:
- How is today similar to the past?
- How is today different from the past?
- How are you different now than you were then?

Discovering what you want:
- What outcome do you want in this situation?
- What can you do to create that outcome?
- How can we help you do that?
- What do you want to do differently in the future?

Naming your black hole:
- What would you like to name this black hole?

Body-Centered Release Questions

Let your fear lead you into a black hole.
- What are you afraid of?
- What are you struggling with?
- How does this pattern serve you?
- How does this pattern limit you?
- What is this pattern most afraid to admit?

Describe your physical sensations.
- Where do you feel afraid in your body?
- What does it feel like?
- What does it look like?

Name your hidden emotions.

- What would be even worse—more frightening, more humiliating?
- Where is this new feeling located in your body?
- Are you noticing any shame, anger, or frustration?
- Who are you angry or frustrated with?
- Is there anyone else you're frustrated, angry with?
- Where is the frustration located in your body? (if any)
- Where is the shame located in your body? (if any)
- Where is the anger located in your body? (if any)
- What does it look and feel like?
- Expand your physical sensations through conscious breathing and physical movement.

Find the lessons learned.

- What message does the released energy have?
- What have you learned?

EXPANDING YOUR BELIEFS

In both the body-centered and the mind-centered release process, you may find a limiting belief that is resistant to change. Beliefs are thoughts that we have retraced in our minds. These beliefs can make it difficult for us to reach beyond our self-imposed limitations. However, we can change our beliefs. To expand and change a belief, find the exact wording of your current belief. A limiting belief is a conviction that you can't do something, that you aren't enough of something, that you can't have something, that life has to be hard, lonely, or limited in some way.

Examples of Limiting Beliefs

- I was born to struggle.
- Never be angry.

- I don't have a clue what to do.
- I'm all alone.
- I'm an outsider.
- The people I love will leave me.
- I can't get what I want in life.
- Others control me.
- I have to please others.
- I'm not safe.
- It's not OK to feel.
- I can never relax.

In order to change a limiting belief, write down the belief that you want to change. Ask yourself what is true on a deeper level. Choose a new belief statement that you want to believe. Choose a statement that feels satisfying to you on a deeper level and write it next to the old belief. Connect them by beginning with the words "Even though I believe..." For example, "Even though I believe that I'm all alone, I am connected to a larger spiritual presence." This is a belief pair.

Awareness of your emotional, mental, physical, and spiritual experience is helpful. Notice the physical and emotional sensations of your old belief as you mentally repeat the belief pair. Invite your spiritual observer to experience the process. State the belief pair repeatedly for a minute or two.

There are a couple of things you can do to accept these phrases in your unconscious mind. While repeating the phrases you can trace an infinity sign (or figure 8 lying on its side) with your eyes, like watching a Ping-Pong match. It's a little easier if someone moves her hand in the shape of an infinity sign in front of you. Have her stand a couple of feet away and wave her arm as if she were conducting a slow waltz. Follow the movement with your eyes while holding your head still. Repeat the phrases for one to three minutes. Stop when you feel they are linked in your experience. The combination of awareness, eye movement, and words keeps your mind from resisting the information. Another activity that can help is to tap just behind your ears. Use your fingers cupped around your ears as though you were putting on earmuffs and tap gently while you repeat the phrases.

Below are examples of belief pairs. I encourage you to develop your own. Exact wording is important and each person's limiting belief and expanded belief statement will be different.

Examples of Belief Pairs

- Even though I believe that I was born to struggle, everything comes to me easily.

- Even though I believe that I can never be angry, I can let people know when I feel angry.

- Even though I believe that I don't have a clue what to do, I do have all my own answers.

- Even though I believe that I'm an outsider, I have a special purpose here.

- Even though some of the people I love will leave, there will always be others to love.

- Even though I believe that I can't get what I want in life, I love and respect myself.

- Even though I believe that others control me, I can do what I want.

- Even though I believe that I have to please others, I love and accept myself.

- Even though I believe that I'm not safe, I can create my own safety.

- Even though I believe that it's not OK to feel, I am both vulnerable and strong.

- Even though I believe that I can never relax, I can let go and be who I am.

TAPPING TO RELEASE EMOTIONAL INTENSITY

If you are afraid of the intensity of your feelings, your body has pressure points that can help you release intense emotional energy. The following are pressure points that help to release some of the more intense emotions. Breathe evenly, keep talking, and look around while you tap these pressure points.

Fear/Anxiety/Stress

People often bring their hands up to their chests when they are frightened. This natural reaction helps the body return to balance.

- Find your collarbone below your neck.
- Let your fingers slide down to the soft area below the collarbone.
- Tap or rub gently on both sides about 3-4 inches apart.

Another stress reliever is to place your hand on your forehead and gently lean into your hand.

Anger/Frustration

Our natural inclination to hold our temples helps release frustration and anger.

- Gently tap or rub the outside edge of your eyebrows on the bone between your eye and your temple.
- Tap on both the left and right together. You can also rub this point with a small circular motion.

Continue as you talk about what has made you angry.

Grief/Sadness/Sorrow

Tap gently on the pressure points on your hand one at a time.

- Turn your hand upright as though you were going to shake hands and point your index finger horizontally.
- Tap on the soft skin next to your fingernail.
- Tap the bottom of your knuckles where your little finger is attached.

Talk about your sorrow as you tap. Our natural inclination to wring our hands actually helps release grief.

Humiliation/Shame/Rejection

We naturally bring our hands up to our faces or hug ourselves when we feel ashamed or rejected. Use three fingers together to tap each point gently on each pressure point.

- Tap just under your nose and above your upper lip.
- Tap just under your lower lip on the middle of your chin.
- Tap on the soft fleshy back side of your underarms one at a time. This area may be a little tender.

Repeat this series until your feelings release a little. Talk about what happened while you tap.

ACTIVITIES THAT HELP RELEASE BLACK HOLES

The following activities can help you release your black holes:

- Individual and group activities such as: walking, running, weight training, hiking, rowing, skiing, rollerblading, yoga, stretching, skating, jumping, dancing, aerobics, paddling, climbing, Frisbee.
- Competitive sports such as: basketball, football, soccer, hockey, tennis, handball, racquetball, rugby, bowling.
- Bodywork such as energy massage, Rolfing, acupuncture, or chiropractic adjustments can loosen up and open the flow of your physical energy. Talk to your practitioner about releasing blocked energy. Find someone who understands energy terminology and flow. Physical adjustments are more likely to remain open when combined with mental understanding and emotional release.

EXPAND YOUR SPIRITUAL ENERGY FIELD

When your black hole has released energy, but has left a void or emptiness, infusing yourself with light will help complete the release. Ask yourself what color of light your body would like. It may be one color like red or blue. It may be two colors like white and purple together. Or it may be a rainbow of colors. Imagine the light flooding into your body and soothing the tension and discomfort. Imagine this light filling the emptiness. Your friends can imagine seeing you in a column of light as you do this. Sometimes it is helpful to have one of your friends put his hand in the center of your back or on your head and imagine light flowing through his hand. This is similar to healing touch, which is practiced in many hospitals.

Any time during the release of a black hole if you feel a little shaky or confused, have one of your friends gently hold your head. Have her place one of her hands gently on your forehead and her other hand behind your head. Her hands should be barely touching you. Allow your head to relax and move freely in her hands for a minute or two. Her hands should follow your movement. This restful holding usually stabilizes the energy in your head so that you can think more clearly.

If your energy is still low, give yourself time and remain mindful of all you are experiencing. Some black holes take more time to release than others.

You may want to trust your dreams to help you understand and accept your black holes. Resuming your usual distractions, working, watching movies, or helping others will help put your black holes back to sleep until they trigger again.

Once in a while the release of a black hole is so powerful that there is an adjustment period of a couple of weeks following the release. The adjustment period can include feeling a little scrambled or lost. You may have headaches or stomach flu-like symptoms. These are adjustments your body is making to accommodate the changes you have made in your energy field. Some people call on chiropractors, massage therapists, acupuncturists, or other body therapists to help with these adjustments. These symptoms usually disappear within a couple of weeks.